"In *Leap Out of Your Lane*, M
advice about how to make t
your life). Pick up a copy n
— **Randi Braun, WSJ Best-Selling Author of** *Something Major: The New Playbook for Women at Work*

"A powerful narrative and compelling read that propels readers to view change as a catalyst for personal and professional growth. Drawing from her family's journey and inspiring stories of others, Lithgow's practical approach offers readers a toolkit for embracing change and unlocking their full potential."
— **Lucy Chen, International Impact Book Award Winning Author of** *Build Resilience: Live, Learn, and Lead*

An inspiring read that will teach you some of life's most important lessons; namely that change is a positive and not a negative, and that success does not necessarily mean optimizing the road that you're already traveling.
— **Melissa Cohen, Founder, Owner MBC Consulting, Co-Founder DIY Influence**

"I loved the real life experiences from her parent's life and her childhood to illustrate that Leaper mentality has to be nurtured throughout one's life. Embracing change early in life showing great opportunities are on the other side of the seemingly insurmountable challenges. A wonderful lesson for us all."
— **Kevin Stephens, Board of Directors, Crown Castle, Consumer Cellular, Keysight**

"Mirna's work will inspire her readers and offer hope that even the most difficult circumstances can be conquered with the appropriate level of faith, self-confidence, determination and hard work."
— **Randy Gromlich, VP, LogixFiber**

"Through Mirna's captivating narrative, readers are drawn into her story, and encouraged to believe in their own capacity for transformation. Lithgow balances sharing her inspiring story while also making the reader feel that change and leaping out of your lane is an attainable goal."
— **Deanna Senior, Founder, Executive Coach, DSS Advisory**

"Mirna Eusebio Lithgow encourages everyone to embrace a Leaper's mindset, empowering us to craft our professional and personal destinies. Mirna's straightforward eight-step approach encourages reflection and prompts a shift towards more fulfilling career trajectories."
— **Sean Ansett, President, At Stake Advisors, Co-Founder Team Member, Fairphone**

"A must-read book for aspiring and current leaders to navigate change with a practical approach. It challenges conventional wisdom, urging readers to rethink their approach to change and risk, in an era where adaptability and resilience are paramount."
— **Dr. Anna Litvak-Hinenzon, PhD, Chief AI Product Officer, ALH.AI**

LEAP OUT OF YOUR LANE

LEAP OUT OF YOUR LANE

THE PLAYBOOK FOR UNLOCKING YOUR SUCCESS BY EMBRACING CHANGE

8 STRATEGIES TO MAKE CHANGE BE YOUR CURRENCY

MIRNA EUSEBIO LITHGOW

MANUSCRIPTS
PRESS

LEAP OUT OF YOUR LANE
The Playbook for Unlocking Your Success by Embracing Change

ISBN

979-8-88504-381-6   *Hardcover*

979-8-88504-380-9   *Paperback*

979-8-88504-379-3   *Ebook*

To my family, my world.

To my husband, Ivan—you are my rock.

Thank you for loving me unconditionally.

To my dear "padres," Elvira and Carlos,

for showing me the path of love and effort.

To my beloved children, Isabella Maria and Ivan Ernesto—

you have shown me the greatest love and blessing.

I'm proud of you.

To my dear sister, Marigina, for all the creative moments

and memories we built together.

I love each one of you with all my heart.

CONTENTS

INTRODUCTION 9

PART I. THE LEAPER'S MINDSET 15

CHAPTER 1. ARRIVAL: THE LEAPER WITHIN 17

CHAPTER 2. HISTORY OF SUCCESS: IT IS NOT A STRAIGHT LINE 29

CHAPTER 3. STATUS QUO: DEBUNKING "IT IS WHAT IT IS" 43

CHAPTER 4. THE SHOWSTOPPER: FEAR AND HOW IT CAN
HOLD YOU BACK 55

PART II. THE LEAPER'S PLAYBOOK 71

CHAPTER 5. THE LEAPER'S PLAYBOOK: EIGHT STRATEGIES TO
EMBRACE CHANGE 73

CHAPTER 6. STRATEGY #1: SELF-AWARENESS AND COMPASSION 87

CHAPTER 7. STRATEGY #2: GRIT AND COURAGE: PASSION,
PIVOT, AND PERSEVERANCE. 97

CHAPTER 8. STRATEGY #3: BEING A CONSTANT LEARNER:
SHIFTING YOUR MINDSET 107

CHAPTER 9. STRATEGY #4: BUILDING RESILIENCE AND SELF-
CONFIDENCE 119

PART III.   LEAPER'S BLUEPRINT   133

CHAPTER 10. STRATEGY #5: A PURPOSE-DRIVEN LIFE   135

CHAPTER 11. STRATEGY #6: TAKE ACTION AND MOVE FORWARD   151

CHAPTER 12. STRATEGY #7: CHANGE AS YOUR LIFESTYLE   167

CHAPTER 13. STRATEGY #8: LEAPER'S CHEERLEADERS: DEFINE
             YOUR TRIBE   181

CONCLUSION   189

ACKNOWLEDGMENTS   195

APPENDIX   199

INTRODUCTION

"The world as we have created it is a process of our thinking. It cannot be changed without changing our thinking."

—ALBERT EINSTEIN

"Hi there, Mirna."

"Hi, Kevin. How are you? It's good to hear from you."

"Listen, I have something important I want to talk to you about. Are you available now?"

This call was in the fall of 2016, when everything changed for my family and a new chapter opened in our lives.

My family of four and I were living in the Dominican Republic, in a cozy house in a suburban complex, and during the most successful moments of our careers as tech executives. It was a Thursday afternoon, with the sun shining and soaking hot outside. While waiting at home to have lunch with my husband, Ivan, I received an unexpected phone call from a colleague in the USA. He asked if I would consider interviewing for a big job in New York City. My brown eyes opened wide, and I looked at myself in the hall mirror. Without hesitation, I responded, "Yes, this is something I can evaluate and explore."

I opened myself to change mine and my family's life—including my husband, my teenage daughter and son, and even our little white Maltipoo, Skipper. We were getting into something totally out of our comfort zone; to start again in a new place and drive ourselves into the unknown.

After landing the job, selecting a school, and finding where to live, we moved to New York.

The expression about New York City, "If you make it here, you make it anywhere," is an understatement. This change was one of the most challenging we have ever experienced, but it was also the most rewarding for our careers, family bonding, and individual development. I took the job and, with it, started a track to greater success: I was promoted within the first year, my husband became a successful executive, we bought a house in New York, and our kids got into their dream US schools.

We also bonded on a different level as a family and opened our kids to a new world of being independent individuals with character, courage, and grit. We saw the world through the lens of two of my favorite phrases: "Not everything has to be perfect to be wonderful," and, "Everything you want is on the other side of fear."

I realized a pattern, where I had often taken a different and more complex path or a new, challenging project or job that pushed me beyond my comfort zone. I opened my mind to exploring it right away simply because, through the years, I had been exposing my family to get out of the comfort zone. And that grit and embracing change had already propelled our careers over and over again.

We all naturally strive for safety and comfort, or to "make the best of a bad situation," and think being successful comes from optimizing the path where you already are. Usually, people like to be an expert in their field, understand a specific swim lane, and dive deep into it. I spent half my career in consumer services, building tech products catering to the consumer market. When I accepted a new challenge, taking on a new segment—managing the entire business market—I excelled and accelerated my career significantly.

We can even see this from the experiences of brave people who dare to try something new or do things differently to get new results. My dear friend and Dominican-born Stephanie Nuesi is a perfect example. Around seven years ago, she had no idea how to write and speak English, she lived in a small town in the Dominican Republic, and her mom worked daily to feed her family going through challenging situations. Stephanie moved with her family to the US and was able to learn English in a public library since they couldn't afford anything else.

While working two jobs to put food on the table for her family and getting rejections from many schools, she got accepted to Baruch College in New York, started a career in Fintech, landed her dream job in one of the Big Tech companies, became the founder and CEO of Max Up to help others develop their careers, and now has more than 250,000 followers and over 150 million views on LinkedIn.

Just imagine: coming from a small rural town in the Dominican Republic, an island in the Caribbean, where she worked hard every day to contribute to feeding the family. In seven years, she accomplished this through a leap of faith and believing she could get there and landed her dream job—through challenging herself to do something new, accepting new opportunities, setting goals, and, as her mom always used to tell her, not settling for less until she made it happen.

How can you apply what you've learned in one lane to excel in a new lane?

Most people believe doing this means exposing themselves to too much risk and that they should be staying in the status quo and with the parts they already know or the careers they already built. Many people think doing the same thing over and over will lead them to become an expert in a category or an industry or become indispensable in one area or field, which can lead them to some level of success. Still, you won't see the next level fast enough, realize your full potential, see your big idea turn into an initial public offering, get that investment from a venture capitalist, or watch your business grow exponentially.

If you are a student who just started your college journey; are in the early stages of your career; have been laid off or don't like your current job; are building a big idea as a startup; are going through your midlife wondering if you chose the right path; or you feel you don't want to miss out on the best chapter of your life story and tremendous success—this book is for you.

After reflecting on my personal experiences and my career journey—facing many obstacles, rejections, moments of uncertainty and loss, and moments of success—and after sitting down with fascinating and successful individuals and researching this topic, I found that greater success comes from leaping into new situations.

I realized throughout the years that building strength to expose yourself to new experiences with courage and determination propels your life, career, and family further. It's about being comfortable with the uncomfortable, finding ways to get out of your comfort zone. You need to build the strength to propose new ideas in unknown areas, contribute to others to avoid silos at work, and make it a lifestyle to embrace change, navigate difficult times, and grasp opportunities that others may pass.

This led me to review the traits and mindsets that others and I have followed to turn change into opportunity.

Let's demystify together the negative connotation that comes with the word "change" to a positive one, reprogramming ourselves to explore more and enjoy our lives to the fullest.

Leapers are change makers and change agents. They see challenges and adjustments as opportunities; as catalysts for growth. They seek change and evolution, embracing them to leave a positive mark in their lives.

You should still have a plan, tools, and the necessary preparation. I am now sharing my eight-step playbook with the strategies to help you leap out of your lane and future-proof yourself to navigate changes successfully. As we advance in our time together, you will learn more about yourself, what could be refraining you from growing or experiencing a joyful life, and what you can do about it now.

I challenge you to embark on this journey with me, learn to apply this framework to leap out of your lane, and experience the life and greater success you deserve.

PART I

THE LEAPER'S MINDSET

CHAPTER 1

ARRIVAL: THE LEAPER WITHIN

"The future belongs to those who believe in the beauty of their dreams."
—ELEANOR ROOSEVELT

On June 24, 2017, we arrived at John F. Kennedy International Airport in New York City on an early morning flight. The warm and breezy weather, with clear blue skies, gave us a refreshing welcome to the United States of America. I set eyes on my family: my husband for the past twenty-two years, Ivan; my twelve-year-old daughter, Isabella; my fifteen-year-old son, Ivan Ernesto; and our little white Maltipoo dog, Skipper. Isabella took Skipper out of the small kennel, his traveling home during the three-hour-and-a-half flight from the Dominican Republic, and hugged him close while putting him on a leash to walk with us through the JFK madness.

From this day on, a new chapter would start for my family, living in a completely different country, without our expanded supportive family structure that included my parents, in-laws, friends, family, and much help from my kid's nanny and housekeeper. We were on our own, just the four of us, with our determination and faith to guide us. Little did we know that would follow this decision. We were being courageous, not by coincidence but by design.

As we exited the customs area with our luggage, we stopped in the middle of the crowded terminal, and my husband looked at us with those green eyes that have been my light for many years and sighed. It felt like time had stopped in the middle of the JFK chaos filled with many people talking in different languages. As they say here, "New York is the true melting pot." As we headed to the Car Rental area on one of the upper floors, my husband stopped, wrapped his arms around us, and said, "Are you guys ready for this adventure? This is it, guys!"

We all looked at him with puzzled faces that quickly turned into big smiles. We all said, almost at once, "We are ready!" I looked back at the three of them and said, "New York, here we come!"

Change stands as an inevitable constant in our lives, and everybody reacts to it differently. Sometimes, it grips us with a jarring sentiment that makes us think negatively about it. The word "change" is usually attached to a negative connotation and associated with fear, when really it is more of an opportunity to recalibrate and move forward.

I looked up the word "change" in the *Merriam-Webster Dictionary*, and surprisingly, there are more than ten definitions and applications. Here are the ones that align with our topic (Merriam-Webster 2023).

Change
Verb—to make different in some particular; to replace with another.

Noun—the act, process, or result of changing such as: alteration, transformation, substitution.

If we take a closer look at the definitions, it has words that could potentially seem frightening and filled with uncertainty to anyone. I found that in the quest to master change, it's crucial to recognize our brains are not inherently designed to handle it well.

As Kasia Jamroz writes in her *Forbes* article,

> The key aim of the brain is survival. Its protective mechanisms keep us alive and got us where we are today, yet they are becoming less effective in today's corporate world. And that is the main problem. Thanks to neuroscience, a field of study that helps us understand how our brain works and the impact of change on its performance, we know today that the brain perceives uncertainty, volatility, ambiguity, and unpredictability the same way as it would when it registers a threat of a lion in the savannah. It activates the exact same part of the brain and triggers the same reaction—an acute stress response (a.k.a. fight or flight response) as if we were faced with an actual life-threatening concern (Jamroz 2019).

Moving is a significant change, and I knew as a family, we had to be all in before taking this step, or this would not work for us. I also knew that throughout the years of our life story—and my upbringing—situations of change and sorting out challenges were always present, especially when we lived in a developing country, and this will help us along the way even though we still had much to go through on our journey.

THE UPBRINGING: BEING OPEN TO SWITCHING LANES

My story of doing things differently and switching lanes goes back to when I was a little girl. My sister was always my accomplice in trying new things and getting out of our comfort zones. I come from a mixed-race household with a black dad and a white mom, and we never saw any issues with their differences. On the contrary, it felt beautiful. We were living in Santo Domingo, the capital city of the Dominican Republic, growing up in the wonderful 1980s and '90s eras. We lived in a cozy middle-class suburban two-story home surrounded by great friends in a neighborhood where we used to play outside, ride bicycles, play volleyball, and listen to music all the time.

I've always had an entrepreneurial spirit and a drive to develop businesses. Even playing games with my sister, I would set up a travel agency, a hospital, or a lemonade stand. I would transform and improve each business to make it different. I sold lemonade and bundled the offering with homemade popcorn.

We would also create popcorn mini bags using wrapping paper and a candle to combine the ends and form perfectly transparent bags of different sizes and prices. We always sold out and started to recruit some of our friends for home delivery in the neighborhood. I now see the popcorn bags on the supermarket shelves and remember my childhood when I anticipated this business.

As a little girl, I also strived to innovate and excel. I had a motivation in me to continue learning and improving. During my middle and high school years, Dad used to ask with a chuckle, "Mirna, why do you get in so much trouble? Can't you use a cardboard presentation for this assignment? Is a video recording necessary?"

"Dad, please, if I can do things differently and better, why wouldn't I? If I can break with what was done before and bring these new tools, the teacher will be impressed! We are the only team doing this. Can you imagine?" I said.

Yeah, I know what you are thinking: A video is a standard practice in any classroom nowadays with all the cell phones and Go-Pros. In the early '90s, audiovisuals were a complicated option to pull off with scarce resources. Despite the challenges this posed to us as students, I encouraged my small group of four to go through the hurdle. After this innovative presentation, the teacher exonerated us from taking the final exam, and we earned an A-plus.

They also selected our video to show at the school library and shared it with all students for a complete week. Our editing skills and tools were limited. We had to show the video on the screen and have an audiocassette playing synchronized on a radio—yep!

We birthed a new standard by doing it. If you can step out of your comfort zone and excel, why not give it a try?

My little sister and I made it our mandate never to settle for the ordinary. Our mom, ever our partner in crime, would help us persuade our dad. She took the initiative to order the video camera and creatively secured the funds to purchase it, despite our family's middle-class budget that didn't easily allow for such expenses.

My mom, Elvira Lithgow, was the first of thirteen siblings in her family to graduate from college and at a time when girls wouldn't consider pursuing a career. I remember the one story of her dad saying, "Elvira, you don't need to go to college. One day, you will marry a man who will take care of you." My mom had a spirit too wild for the cage of expectations, and her response was, "Dad, I want to study and do things differently. I want a career, to be independent, to help and go work for a company." This didn't stop her. Moving to the city, she took refuge in a relative's home, a modest outpost on her journey to autonomy, and worked two shifts to pay for her school expenses.

She would then go and walk for miles to get to her school with just one pair of shoes. She juggled work and study until she graduated with high honors, got a job in telecommunications as an operator, and continued growing until she reached the management role she wanted and provided for her family. We have her example of determination of getting things done and going against all odds and obstacles; persevering for what we believed in, even if that seemed impossible to others; but most importantly, not having any hesitation for defying the odds and pivoting.

My parents met and got married while working for a telecommunications company. I guess I can be called a "Baby Telco." As I grew up and started my professional life, my mother provided many amazing examples of what an effective leader is. She genuinely cared for her people, defined clear and challenging goals for them, celebrated successes, and took advantage of every opportunity to turn it into personal growth and achievement. Until this day, I get many compliments from her former employees and colleagues on how she leads through empathy, kindness, accountability, and passion. My mom has always been one of the funniest people I know, even at work.

Our Mom always says, "Inspiration to others is best achieved by leading by example. That's why you need to set your standards high, strive for excellence, and leave your mark." We will deep dive in part three of the book into how to make this your own lifestyle when you create your blueprint.

In her retirement years, she keeps leaping out, empowering men and women by starting a "Club of Elderly Walkers" and becoming their president. More than that, this elderly community cherishes her because she has provided them with goals, vision, and unforgettable fun activities that keep them moving and inspired. Her next leap is writing a book, despite being in her eighties!

Dad also has a story about perseverance and hard work, being the oldest sibling in his family who started to work at a very young age to help bring food to their table. He spent almost thirty-two years reaching a management position in Telecom Engineering and then leaping out years later to build his own company and become an entrepreneur. I recall stories from when Hurricane David hit the island—the strongest and deadliest to go through the Dominican Republic—and he walked out of our small house in the city, leaving us secured, and joined a small group of engineers and technicians who kept communications afloat despite category five winds and wreckage all around.

During the rhythm of our middle and high school years, our living room often transformed into a stage, watching music videos on the television with my sister to learn every move, from Janet Jackson's iconic "Rhythm Nation" to Debbie Gibson's "Electric Youth" to one of my favorites that had us striking poses, Madonna's hit "Vogue," spinning to the vibrant Gloria Estefan's "Turn the Beat Around." We also danced to the unforgettable "Bidi-Bidi-Bom-Bom" by Selena and the Dominican beats of Merengue from Juan Luis Guerra "Viene a Pedir mi Mano." We love music. Dancing is a passion for us, and we created the biggest choreographies seen at our school. We were trendsetters and turned this into a movement!

In the following years, we were the headliners for every show at school, recruiting entire classes and even overseeing executing new ideas. We also came up with a fashion show that became a tradition in other schools, and we were called in as consultants… two kids still fourteen and sixteen years old. These events were unprecedented. We transformed the traditional fundraisers like field days and selling food for the school senior class fundraiser.

FINDING A NEW PATH TO ACHIEVE YOUR GOALS
According to new research, there have been notable shifts in entrepreneurs in the United States shifting to an older demographic, with a decrease of younger entrepreneurs.

"We have seen a notable shift toward older new entrepreneurs. In 1996, 14.8 percent of entrepreneurs were 55–64 years old, compared to 22.8 percent in 2021. At the same time, we have seen a decrease in the share of younger new entrepreneurs; according to research from the Ewing Marion Kauffman Foundation, "Who is the Entrepreneur? New Entrepreneurs in the United States, 1996–2021" (Kauffman Foundation 2022, 3).

Is this entrepreneurship spirit now postponed to a later time in life? Is it fear of economic instability or failure? Has the entrepreneurial spirit been quieted early on in our lives by the noise around us to keep with the established path and the "secure job" that is not secure anymore? If we look at sectors such as tech, which used to presume the long live career traditionally, they are now adjusting to post-pandemic years by doing massive layoffs, and according to MarketWatch, more than 240,000 people have been impacted as of October 2023, which results in a 50 percent increase since 2022 numbers (Rogers 2023).

You don't need to stick to the established path or what proved as successful before. There is always room for setting your unique path to growth and innovation. We will work together on this further in Believing in Your Definition of Success.

You can course-correct at any given time. You have the power to decide to make a change, no matter how many times others try to convince you otherwise. Don't let them get in your head. Look deep inside for what you believe is true, and give it all you can to accomplish your goal.

This new chapter for my family, starting our new lives in New York, was a continuation of how I lived my life, doing things differently and saying yes to challenges I had no clear idea how to solve. We had a plan for the biggest leap in our lives. We also had to be all in, or it would not work.

But how do we do that? How would we stay true to ourselves and what we believe in but also blend in and excel in this Big Apple city? I know now we underestimated how big of a change this consisted of… but does it matter after we decide? A decision is ours to own, like it is our child.

We exited the airport in a rental SUV, and the midday sun cast a glow on the dashboard, an illuminated welcome as we navigated the unfamiliar highways to Long Island. This would be our new home. We had researched the area and knew very little of it then. Our destination was a town called Jericho, right in the middle of the island and about fifty minutes east of NYC by train or, as Long Islanders call it, the LIRR (Long Island Rail Road).

We selected this town because it was closer to my new office and the school district, which ended up being the number one school district in the US the following year. This decision started to feel right already. There were many unknowns, and little did we know what we would encounter next.

Was it easy? No, it certainly was not. Leaping out of your lane will not make this easier or harder. It's about taking the lead in your life and career, exposing yourself and giving permission to the alternative life you can have in your story. Take intentional and conscious steps and adapt your plan as opportunities arise.

My mom always told me, "Mirna, you must be the main character of your movie. The cast is remembered, but the main character is the one remembered the most. Take control of your life and lead the way." She will also say to this day, "Leave your mark everywhere you go. Wherever your name is, in whichever work you deliver, and despite who you deliver it to or who you are talking to, big or small, do it with this special high-quality seal." I live by these words of advice from my mom and strive to become the better version of myself every day.

A better version of yourself will come when you are open to new situations, learn from your mistakes and ventures, bring more self-awareness, give yourself some grace, and learn how to pivot when necessary.

Throughout my childhood and work life, I have seen friends or colleagues thinking the same way or doing the same job for years and years to come, and they are in the same place in their way of thinking or what they do as when I left them twenty years ago. Nothing is wrong with this if that is all you want and have ever dreamed of.

If you are saying, "Well, it is what it is!" I challenge you to ask yourself, "Is it?"

Embracing change is essential for us to thrive. Nevertheless, our brains are wired for routine, favoring the familiar over the unfamiliar, making change harder. An article by Nicole Spector, on NBC News, struck me. The renowned Dr. Sanam Hafeez explained that the brain is protective, often perceiving change as a threat, which can be challenging to overcome. However, it is essential to teach the brain to adapt to change to maintain cognitive health and delay aging. This involves cognitive rehabilitation exercises, learning new skills, and pushing beyond comfort zones, which helps adaptability, boosts confidence, and wards off cognitive decline (Spector 2018).

"Most people won't try something new because they're deathly afraid of failing," notes Hafeez. "When you see that something is doable, it makes you more receptive and braver. That emotional, therapeutic factor is separate from the neural pathway factor. Over the years, we learn to succeed by viewing our previous failures and successes in a certain light, and as we get older we lose sight of that. When you try a new thing, it makes you more confident to try to do more new things."

The alternative I found throughout my life and researching the amazing career journeys of other successful leaders is that at one point in their lives, they were able to expose themselves to new situations, new challenges, or unforeseen circumstances. But they said yes and leaped. Others have designed it—as I've done for myself and my family. By being open to changing lanes and starting something entirely new, you can unlock the potential you always had but were unaware of.

That's when I realized a new mindset had taken hold—a leaper's mindset.

When I took that call in the fall of 2016, I decided once again to leap out of my lane and change my life, challenging myself to beat the unknown, and it has worked wonders for me and my family. I know it will change your life, too. You must believe in the power in you to embrace, navigate, and conquer change.

Make change your currency and make it work in your favor by learning how to leap out to the life you never thought you had in front of you.

As I started my professional career, I made a projection for the first twenty years through a human resources exercise at one of my initial jobs in telecommunications. Will I stay in the same place for twenty or thirty years as my parents did in the baby boomer generation? Would this be the life ahead of me? Would I play it safe and follow a path of becoming that subject matter expert in one field? Or will I reach success through a different path and achieve even greater success?

I knew I wanted a career in management to get the discipline and foundation to eventually start my own company. I opened myself to the challenges I would face, and my choices would take me on this exciting journey to achieve even more.

Our life and career paths to success are not linear. As we continue this journey of self-discovery, we will analyze why this is important now, more than ever with the volatility in the markets, as a critical skill for students, rising leaders, and managers at all levels and stages in their lives. I will dive deeper into what it takes and will provide you a guide to define your own blueprint to get there. Most important is to make this a lifestyle your natural state to live through the endless changes in your world with the right toolkit to face them.

Leaper's Tip

When we open ourselves to the possibility of change and start to see it as a positive instead of a negative in our lives, a whole new world of opportunities opens. Let's review this together.

- How has your upbringing influenced where you are now related to embracing change?

- Start an inventory of moments where you could try something new, or there was an opportunity to take a different path.

- Briefly analyze the thought process that took you to the final decision and course of action.

- Was the outcome part of your initial plan? Did you course correct if needed, or drag along?

- How comfortable do you feel with changes that come your way?

CHAPTER 2

HISTORY OF SUCCESS: IT IS NOT A STRAIGHT LINE

———————

"Where you start should not determine where you end."

—GINNI ROMETTY, FORMER IBM CEO

START OF A JOURNEY

On a warm Santo Domingo day in 1998, I could melt away during the summertime when there was no breeze in the air or a shade in sight. It was late afternoon, and Ivan had just proposed to me in a romantic dinner setting. I said yes! One of the most transformational moments is becoming a new entity where you form a new family. And one of the most important decisions in our lives is to select the person who will be our partner through that journey we call life. Ivan had just been promoted to manager in his new job at a large retailer IT department, and I had a marketing analyst job at Verizon, one of the largest telecommunicators in DR. After six years of dating, it felt like the right moment and time.

We arrived at my parent's cozy apartment located in one of the central suburbs of the city to tell them the news and celebrate.

"We're so happy for you, Ivan and Mirna!" my mother said.

"Let's open a bottle of champagne to celebrate!" my dad said. We heard a *pop!* and he served five glasses, including my sister's.

"We're so happy too! I need to start the planning, Mom, and will need all the help in the world," I said, bursting with happiness—my sparkling eyes and big smile showed. The excitement and happiness were real. We had been boyfriend and girlfriend for the past six years, and we had set a date to marry a year from that night.

My husband has been my rock and oasis. We complement each other well and have been madly in love since my senior year in high school. He is organized and meticulous. Sometimes I tell him he's like Monica from *Friends* with how much he wants to clean and keep things in order. I live my life more relaxed when needed due to juggling multiple activities and our demanding work life. He has supported me in every career transition and decision to try something new. He has been there in the moments of truth and picked me up when I needed to start from scratch.

From being a "door-to-door" mobile phone sales representative to a senior vice president of a $10 billion company, I knew the road would be much harder without him and the support structure around me.

I based my career progression on taking new challenges or projects that require profound transformation and when, in many cases, few were eager to take them. But I did.

I took on challenging situations or even projects on top of my regular responsibilities and excelled at them. I learned to master the foundation, resilience, and focus and feel comfortable with the uncomfortable.

You can too.

I also mapped out my career journey for the next twenty years and what I wanted through a human resources exercise. Then, I put words into action, constantly mastering one job to start seeking the next level or moving to a new department or project. Moving up the corporate ladder and doing all these challenges come with a big warning: Once you have something figured out and mastered, you enter a *comfort zone*. Getting out of it is hard and contrary to your nature of a stable and steady progression.

The expected path is learning and mastering a task, a job, or a process and being extremely good at it or even becoming a subject matter expert. Nothing is wrong with having it all figured out and climbing the corporate ladder slowly but steadily in one area of expertise. This path is common.

We feel safe becoming this subject matter expert and going through a known pattern. We also start to feel indispensable, that we know all these things and are key to the company. This will eventually get you stuck, as I have seen from different mentees who expressed not being able to grow. You are setting your own trap, and your boss will never let you leave that quickly to other opportunities that bring you career progression.

What I found throughout experiences of my own and other top executives is that new projects that are cross-functional and out of your scope, or even in a newly created strategic unit or division no one understands yet, are the ones that give you the maximum exposure and opportunity to grow and excel. Don't get me wrong, everything comes with a level of risk. It is through this calculated risk that turns it into an opportunity instead of an adverse situation to avoid.

Do you want to do the same every day for the rest of your life, just mastering what you already know? Are you comfortable where you are now, and that's it for you? Do you even like what you are doing now or have been doing for a while? Is your passion elsewhere and you feel you must do what is expected from you instead of following your dream? Do you want to keep silos in your organization?

I don't think so. And deep inside, you don't either.

BECOMING A LEAPER

As a leaper, I seek new challenges and make "change" my currency.

If not, I get bored and feel stalled!

At this point you should be wondering, Who do we call a leaper?

A leaper sees the world through change, seeks change, and transforms any situation where change is involved into an opportunity.

Leapers are masters of uncertainty. They are flexible, adaptable, curious, focused, and have a growth mindset. They manage to start from scratch or rebuild in challenging situations and moments of crisis and even come back stronger than ever.

Whoever has been a part of telecom, cable, and media companies know how much change occurs in this space, from mergers and acquisitions to restructures, exponential growth, and the ever-changing tech landscape. My parents both worked in telecommunications, which is one of the reasons I chose this path. The other main reason is its impact on improving our lives and the well-applied transformation it can bring to the world.

At the time, my love for technology made me curious enough to take a computer CPU, open it up, disassemble the motherboard and circuits, and put it back together just by reading manuals and asking my dad for his solder to patch a circuit. I had several summer jobs and internships as an operator for messaging dispatch—a sort of WhatsApp at the time—done through an operator that inputs messages on a terminal. I also did door-to-door sales of mobile devices, services, and pagers, and helped my dad with his company's administrative and accounting tasks.

My formal career began in 1996 at Verizon International as a marketing analyst for long distance and toll-free services. During the next ten years, I held several positions, escalating from analyst to manager to senior manager. I moved from long distance voice services to calling cards, then internet services and mobile services. This gave me a 360-degree view of the business. When Verizon's new corporate planning and strategy department started, I applied and got the promotion, being the ideal candidate to help shape the future vision.

If I had stayed in one place or one lane, not taking these changes as opportunities that helped me escalate even faster within the organization, this promotion would have been more difficult to attain, or I would have needed more drive and confidence to do it.

Fast forward to the early 2000s, and my boss Randy, the corporate planning director and expat coming from Verizon headquarters in Dallas, Texas, called me into his office one afternoon and told me, "Mirna, a new project is coming from Verizon headquarters to deploy in every affiliate. It involves frequent interactions with them, and they want to impact a big part of the company's processes. It will require all departments of the company to work differently."

I looked at him straight in the eyes while I felt a big knot in my stomach—the imposter syndrome kicking in. Then I said, to my own surprise, "It sounds like something I want to be a part of, Randy. I can do this!" *I haven't come this far to play chicken now,* I heard one of the voices in my head saying. "I agree, and I definitely think you should take this opportunity and that you'd be great at it." Randy clasped my hands excitedly.

I could have easily remained in my old position: being on the top of my game producing great money, and my position being key to the company and not going away any time soon—a stable moment of success.

However, I learned from Randy the kind of leader I wanted to become for my team, who believes in their team's potential and encourages them to try something new. I identify him as a leaper, open to opportunities and new ideas. He also had taken a leap coming to the Dominican Republic from the US, moving his family to a different country and culture.

This first challenge tasked me with driving a transformation on a larger scale across the entire organization. It required rebuilding the processes, adapting the organization's governance, and restructuring. Together, we were able to turn around the development process, automate deliverables via web portals, and improve the go-to-market playbooks for the entire company. This positively impacted the results and drove over 78 percent improvement in time-to-market.

It also brought benefits into my career, such as exposure to the C-level and training for more than three hundred collaborators at all levels company-wide. This helped me understand the product role from a 360-degree perspective and build transferable skills I mastered to combine them all and use them in my next challenge.

SETBACKS, BURNOUT, AND LEAPS

My career, and almost anyone else, was not a straight line. I was always moving to a new challenge, making a lateral move, and taking on different responsibilities that were helping me become a stronger professional and a better leader.

Years later, as I became a manager and continued to escalate into more senior positions, I forgot how these opportunities can also take a toll on you if you are unprepared, and I burnt out after having my second child. I lost more than forty pounds of weight (some will not complain about this, but it's not a great feeling, trust me), and I could barely eat without feeling my stomach sick. I was seen several times in the hospital for being unwell with fever, flu, you name it. My auto-immune system was telling me, "Enough."

This new experience of managing people surprised me, and I underestimated the needed preparation.

After ten incredible years, I felt a special calling to step down—I could explain in an entirely new book—and decided to step back, recharge, and dedicate myself to being a mom for a while. They offered me a one-year sabbatical and called me crazy to leave at the highest peak of my career, almost at a director level. I appreciated all the C-level execs who took the time from their busy agendas to talk, urging me to reconsider my departure and stay.

I prayed and left it all behind. On a February morning in 2006, in the HR head's office, I resigned with no bad blood. After the meeting, I gathered my things in disbelief that I had done it and then drove home. After all those years, I could feel a strange and bittersweet moment, but it felt right.

My career is over! I thought.

It was far from over.

"I am happy you made this decision, and I've been praying for it," my husband confided back home. His chuckle chased his following words, "I also know you, and I'm sure you will have three signed projects in less than six months."

"I probably will. I don't know. I know this will be a new beginning and allow me to spend more time with the kids," I said.

And I certainly did. They needed me—two and five years old—at the start of life's great adventure, and using this time to create a special bridge of communication and bonding with them helped us in the moments when things get tougher. And I needed them to remind me through all these emotions that every ending is a disguise for a new dawn.

This time allowed me to create the unwavering foundations for Isabella and Ivan that would stand through all their tomorrows, working hard in their studies and focusing on being high achievers and independent. We always found a way to balance our professional lives with raising healthy and responsible young adults—not an easy task and a perfect job, especially for working parents. It required a support system and having many people around us to help us along the way. I'm forever grateful to my parents, family, and caregivers.

During the year 2006, and as my husband predicted, I started several business projects.

At first, I launched a customer service audits and training company with my mother. Then with my sister Marigina, we launched the biggest girls' summer camp in DR for ages three to fifteen, focused on empowering girls through fun and enriched activities with over four thousand participants within the following ten years. The third project, a skill I developed and worked on with my sister-in-law, specialized in call center deployments, which would help me in one of my following leaps.

Each business had a new area that allowed the entrepreneur in me to flourish, provided for my family, and helped me learn about doing more with fewer resources, which prepared me for my next challenge.

The leaper in me created a method to master changes in my life, and this last burnout showed me that being intentional is important; being prepared as a leaper is even more critical.

THE SCARCITY EFFECT VERSUS MINDSET

Over the next three years, the projects were growing quickly. Keeping up with the three businesses turned out rewarding but also time-consuming. Being an entrepreneur has its advantages: the learnings and the constant need to become creative despite the scarce resources to make this venture flourish.

If you work for a company with the big bucks, sometimes you lose perspective of that sense of "scarcity."

According to the *Merriam-Webster Dictionary*, "Scarcity" comes from the adjective "scarce," which is defined as "not plentiful or abundant" (Merriam-Webster 2023).

Over the past decade, there has been a lot of academic research around this concept, as cited in "Scarcity: A Consumer Decision Making," an article by Kelly Goldsmith, Vlad Griskevicius, and Rebecca Hamilton for the *University of Chicago Press Journals* and sponsored by the *Journal Association of Consumer Research*. As research on scarcity has evolved, four distinct perspectives on the effects have emerged mainly after COVID-19: resource scarcity (mindset), environmental uncertainty (threat), social comparison (reference point), and choice restriction (a journey) (Goldsmith et al. 2020, 358).

Usually, this word has a negative connotation drawing from the theory of having a "scarcity mindset." I want to challenge this and give it a new meaning for us, and this is to look at scarcity as an effect from the lens of frugality and creativity. The scarcity effect is learning how to do more with less, improvising and finding ways to partner with others to strengthen your position and prioritize.

The scarcity effect helps you sharpen your skills to be frugal, prioritize better, and extract the most out of the assets or enablers you have in hand. This is not about adopting a scarcity mindset. It's about seeing the opportunity behind changes in your environment, current assets, and resources availability, and thinking outside the box to deliver and drive growth.

THE TURNAROUND: BACK TO THE FUTURE OF CABLE AND TELECOM

Telecom and cable kept calling me to come back to work for them. In 2008, I accepted an offer to join the second-largest provider of telecommunication services in DR as director of marketing for residential and business customers. However, since this company had filed for chapter eleven bankruptcy, many people questioned my choice to join them. One of my best friends and mentor called me. "Are you out of your mind? This company filed for chapter eleven. They failed to deliver the returns after the IPO and are in trouble. That will be a big turnaround you will all have to make!"

I stayed silent for a couple of seconds, thinking my words through. I didn't want to sound overly optimistic. A decision like this needs careful review, and I reached my decision. "Transformation is my wheelhouse, and I never had this experience before. It will be something new and complex that I will learn and master." I already had a family with two kids and a mortgage, which made the decision harder. I sighed and continued, "I believe in this executive team. Something special is happening here, and I love becoming a part of it."

I recently connected with their former CEO, who helped navigate the process after filing for chapter eleven. He reminded me that Tricom had accumulated significant successes at the beginning of its existence, becoming a benchmark in the telecommunications sector in Central America and the Caribbean. The company broke the monopoly that had prevailed over six decades in the Dominican Republic; introduced products that revolutionized the market, such as prepaid cell phones; and attracted global-level investors like Motorola—the first-ever Dominican company to conduct an IPO.

Now, I was leading the transformation of the product portfolio and fueling growth back into the business. This massive transformation spanned several organizations, including product, marketing, and communications, while managing a delicate P&L with limited resources that strained every department.

The first day of work had arrived, and I met with Waldo, the VP of finance—not a shocker. He is a sharp and witty guy with a great sense of humor. Waldo, who could pierce through the most tangled financial webs with a clever quip, wanted to make things more evident about what I signed up for. As I entered his office on the third floor of the headquarters building, I noticed it turned out much smaller than I expected.

"Come on in, Mirna." He pointed to one of the only two chairs in front of his desk. "So nice that you have decided to join us in this transformation quest. I have heard wonderful things about you, and we need all the help we can get in this process."

"Let me walk you through financials," he said. "This is the budget, and just for you to know how critical your unit is for the company, if your unit catches a cold… the company gets pneumonia."

No pressure, I thought. *We are in a company going through chapter eleven. What were you expecting, Mirna?*

"Marketing expense doesn't seem that bad. I've seen smaller. I can work with this," I said. We had a similar budget at Verizon, and curiosity struck me about how they could afford this amount.

"Just to be clear," Waldo continued, "this is the budget expense for the entire year."

I thought it was just one month of expense!

"Oh… I see, Waldo, you know this is a low budget." I then thought about why I was there: to take this challenge and make it work, leaving my mark.

I shook his hand and said, "Let's do it. We will kill it out there!" *Bring it on. This challenge surpasses what I had expected.*

I know what you are thinking. How does this one end?

The bonding and trust of the leadership team was equivalent to a "band of brothers."

As I reflect on these experiences and from my interview with Ryan, their CEO at the time, trust was the first value I could distinguish around the new executive team across the different levels. Employees even voted and accepted not having their bonuses paid that year to ensure the company would survive. That is where I learned the power of trust and what the will of an organization could do when you listen and work together with all levels of the company.

Also, the formality was way different, and how you could access top executives was easy and natural. As a team we would always go in the trenches and meet the employees and customers in the stores, the field services teams, and the engineers building our products. Not only were we able to get the company out of bankruptcy—with multiple achievements, repositioning ourselves, and emerging from the ashes with increased brand awareness and consideration—we doubled the internet customer base and the cable TV subscribers.

In 2011, fifteen months after the company got approval out of chapter eleven, they sold to new management that did a massive restructuring in a cost-cutting move, and we found most of us on the executive level cut. It was a bittersweet moment after how much we had accomplished, and this reality was hitting home. I am thankful for learning how that process feels, a sentiment echoed globally in the aftermath of the layoffs post COVID-19.

There are several key takeaways, and one is that when you have an opportunity to leap to an unknown territory, you grasp it intentionally, knowing it will serve your purpose and add to the building blocks in your career or life journey. Be intentional about it.

Another takeaway is that scarcity can mislead us to have a finite mindset, and we have to carefully visualize it more as an opportunity for us to become assertive. As a leaper, we can learn to create abundance from what we have and differentiate ourselves. We are always seeking to have all the resources at our disposal, but it's not the case every time.

The most important lesson is that having a job doesn't define you, and being laid off doesn't define you either, nor does your level of success.

In fact, according to an article from Zippia more than 40 percent of Americans have been laid off or terminated from a job at least once (Flynn 2023).

You will become a stronger person from change. You must go through it and master as well as others, preparing you to be a better professional and a better person. Also, most importantly, your definition of success is different from others. We will dive deep into this later in the book. This experience positioned me in the market and put me on the road to my next successful chapter.

My career has not been a straight line, and it never will be.

Leaper's Tip

Your career or life journey is not a straight line, and you should be intentional about your leaps. Here are some questions to help you build a foundation to be a leaper.

- Have you defined what your next ten years look like?
- Have you considered where you are now and where you want to be, short- and long-term?
- Make an inventory of your latest career moves.
- Which skills do you believe you have gained? (If you are unsure, ask others in your trust circle, and they will tell you.)

CHAPTER 3

STATUS QUO: DEBUNKING "IT IS WHAT IT IS"

"If you don't like something, change it. If you can't change it, change your attitude."

—MAYA ANGELOU.

NEW BEGINNINGS, STARTING FROM SCRATCH

I started to get calls from other Telcos that wanted me to join their executive teams, and I also took some time off to recharge, spend the holidays with family, create memories together, and have time to rethink my vision. I interviewed with Armand, the VP of business at the second largest mobile provider operated by Orange/France Telecom. He is a highly regarded business executive, and to this day, I call him my friend and a great boss. They wanted me to build their data portfolio for businesses with only a team of one—me.

After briefly discussing it with the human resources teams and negotiating my package, I took the job offer. I hit the ground running and started getting involved in multiple projects, adapting to the team well and starting a transformation across departments and with new products to launch to the market.

After the first year, we started to have tremendous growth as a company. After multiple positions and projects successfully launched, I created a new revenue stream for the company. Fast forward several years, the same holding group acquired this company and the one I worked for before. I knew both companies well, which became an advantage for me during several restructuring rounds in 2015.

The completion of the project marked a turning point, not just for the business but for my trajectory. In the wake of our success, the exhilaration of a new challenge stood tall. Rebuilding the business team was now my responsibility. As I stepped into the role of head of the entire business-to-business unit, I felt excitement course through my veins. There was a profound sense of achievement, a vibrant thread of pride weaving through my professional fabric.

I became the first woman in the country to manage such a structure in Telecom, an honor and a humbling nod to the strides we were making to inclusivity and diversity. Reporting directly to the CEO, I embraced the magnitude of this milestone with pride, ready to move ahead with determination and respect for the path that lay before me. This represented my advocacy for women's leadership with a renewed commitment to open opportunities to other women and pave the way for the new generation.

I made it to the C-suite level and thrived!

We took the business to the highest growth levels. Still, most importantly, I received a broken organization with negative employee satisfaction. Two years later, it had the highest employee satisfaction, net promoter score, and double-digit revenue growth. I looked at the plan I had created at the start of my career and felt such a pleasant joy at reaching another milestone! The leaper's traits helped me tremendously, as well as the opportunity of having been part of a turnaround before and the blessing of conforming a star team.

LEAPER'S MINDSET AND SILOS IN ORGANIZATIONS

In this last leap, I learned that silos can be a massive deterrent in organizations, and people can be protective of the areas they mastered and do a lot of gatekeeping, holding information, and having resistance to new ideas from other areas. The phrase "It is what it is" can be heard everywhere, and it is good to know where you are, but leaders were stuck in the status quo and "this is how we do things from years ago."

I used empathy and trust to create an environment of collaboration between teams to show each other the value of working together to recruit other areas as allies and make them part of our shared mission in the business team. As part of the improvements in my new position, I implemented a new product development process that involved all stakeholders, such as engineering, marketing, products, sales, and support areas. It's the best example of how we all rooted for each other: The engineering team bonded uniquely with the marketing and product team, and we created positive impact for the company.

A leaper's purpose is to look at the big picture and help others see it, too, leaping out to learn other parts of the business that will position them to win and be better at their current roles. That is the power of challenging the status quo and fixed mentalities.

The difference in the success of this leap is that it's all about being intentional and not just doing job-hopping or climbing the corporate ladder. This can happen to you several times within your journey— career or personal life—to decide on taking a complex road or one least traveled.

As featured by *The Economic Times* in a 2023 article, "Midlife Career Change Doesn't Have to Be a Crisis: Time to Debunk Four Career Change Myths," Gen Zers and millennials are more prone to change jobs than Gen Xers and boomers. Why do the risks or fear of changing careers have to hinder your goals or new ambitions? It is time to rethink this statement and be open to new possibilities, despite your age group or situational status (Tandon 2023).

BREAKING FROM THE ORDINARY

This is how I was discovered and offered a job in New York.

I started working for French companies and traveled to many impressive places in Europe such as Paris, Portugal, Romania, and Spain. Learning new cultures is also a passion of mine. In August 2016, as the head of business services then, I had to fly to France from the Dominican Republic, and every affiliate head also flew there for the quarterly review.

I love Paris and the beauty of France—the breathtaking look over the Seine and the Trocadero, the couples sitting on a blanket at Champ De Mars overseeing the Eiffel Tour, the jambon et fromage sandwich and the crème brûlée… all of it. I'm always fascinated and find something new on every trip. I flew with the head of communications during this time, and we arrived in Paris on a Sunday afternoon. Apart from the quarterly review, we had a press conference to announce launching the business-to-business global team, presided over by the CEO and the global head of B2B.

After the press conference, we decided to have dinner for deeper engagement with fellow executives, including the president of business services in the US, Kevin. The restaurant was buzzing with life. Every corner was a testament to the city's ceaseless pulse. We sat along one of the longest tables, immersed in the clink of cutlery and the low murmur of strategic conversations. As the evening unfolded, our dialogue wove through courses. It led to the scheduling of a visit to the company's headquarters the next day, where we would collaborate with the sales and marketing head, aiming to share insights and set benchmarks.

And that's where it happened.

When I asked Kevin why he considered me for the opening in New York, he said, "Mirna, remember that meeting in Paris after the press conference?" I nodded.

He said, "Mirna, you were the only one who went to the Paris office to meet with the local team and also the only one asking good questions."

> Every new experience and connection can present itself as just an experience, or it can be seen as an opportunity that will potentiate your future growth.

Every executive I interviewed or have been around had those moments and grasped them.

You never know who you'll meet—even in the supermarket.

Leapers are always ready. They always give their best and stand out from the ordinary.

The same year we moved to the US, I was featured in *Forbes* magazine as one of DR's fifty most influential women for my work launching a startup hub and achievements in my telecommunications career (Mejia 2017). At that moment, I had to take it all in.

All this happened with so many challenges and mountains I had to climb while raising my kids, trying to attend school presentations and science fair projects. In my case, the struggles many working moms experience are augmented by being between countries.

This experience gave me new skills I could use in any industry, market, or purpose I chose.

Still, why do we doubt when we see an opportunity not in our wheelhouse, in another department, or in a new industry?

Why, in your midlife, don't you feel fulfilled and stay in the same job or build the same career path?

Why do we want to start our next big idea but let the entrepreneur in us die?

I know what you are thinking and the expression that comes after is: "It is what it is." We understand following the path expected of us is the safest way to succeed and that challenging the status quo is too risky.

THERE IS NO SUCCESS WITHOUT STRUGGLE

The idea of changing course or following a different path is not easy, I have to admit.

My mom told me this story once, and I made it into a poem to share:

A Small Boat

A small boat in the middle of a storm,
with no instruments to guide it through,
wondering are we halfway, at the start,
will the high seas let us make it through?

Closer will be the sun to shine over it,
kept going without giving up,
with hope in its chest;
the skies cleared out, and indeed,
at the very end, the boat made it through.

Imagine if, in this story, they would have turned back or given up.
Don't ever give up. The sun can be an inch from shining over you.

Every struggle, every step we climb on the ladder, and
every turn we make will bring troubles and uncertainty
and will also bring the hope of a brighter tomorrow.

I took the process of forming diamonds from a *Smithsonian* magazine
article by Cate Lineberry, "Diamonds Unearthed," where diamond
expert Jeffrey Post explains, with plain and clear words, the genesis
of these rare crystals:

> Diamonds are formed deep within the Earth about 100 miles or
> so below the surface in the upper mantle. Obviously in that part
> of the Earth it's very hot. There's a lot of pressure, the weight of
> the overlying rock bearing down, so that combination of high
> temperature and high pressure is what's necessary to grow dia-
> mond crystals in the Earth (Lineberry 2006).

The beauty of our struggles is like how diamonds are made. They must go through fire and extreme temperatures and rise from the deep. This natural phenomenon mirrors the essence of authentic leadership—the capacity to withstand adversity, embrace the heat of challenge, and hold the weight of responsibility. Character is forged in the depths of tribulations, and resilience is crystalized, bringing clarity and strength like these enduring gemstones.

> Like the formation of diamonds, struggles will make us stronger, more unique, and more beautiful.

We experienced it with the COVID-19 pandemic and how our perceptions—after going through trauma, uncertainty, and despair—shifted how people think about their careers. A study conducted by Onepoll.com for Universal Technical Institute (UTI) on career change explored how COVID-19 had impacted people's next steps in their career choices.

> Conducted in November 2020, the research revealed that 42 percent of Americans had a 'career lightbulb' moment during the pandemic. It also found more than half (53 percent) were looking for a new job that would allow them to avoid ever stepping foot in an office again (Universal Technical Institute 2020).

These findings indicate a paradigm shift in the American workforce, with a discerning emphasis on redefining career paths and preferences considering a post-pandemic world. The mindset shifted after going through a tough situation and becoming stronger.

Before moving to New York, our kids continued school in Santo Domingo until mid-June 2017, and my husband worked as the deputy CIO of a large company and started to transition from that job while finding a new one in the US. I decided to stay present at home somehow while starting to travel to work in my new role.

I spent almost six months flying back and forth from New York to Santo Domingo every week.

The Delta flight 4698 became my second home and where I could feel relaxed after a week of meetings and presentations. My typical week consisted of taking the Monday 6:00 a.m. flight to JFK, renting a car and arriving by noon directly into a meeting in the office, and checking in at the hotel around 8:00 p.m. after an exhausting day. After a long week of hard work, on Thursday night I flew back to SDQ-Santo Domingo on a 6:00 p.m. flight to spend the weekend with my family.

I noticed the flight attendants were starting to recognize me, and I recognized them. *Is this too much now? Why am I doing this?* Without a doubt, it is one of the most challenging things I have ever done, especially being a mom.

I learned to be stronger by myself on some weekends. I would stay in New York, go to church alone, buy groceries, and spend every day soaking in my new environment at a cozy boutique hotel in Woodbury on the Long Island area, my home for six months of intense traveling.

Each day I returned to the hotel, it became a ritual to witness a radiant bride stepping out from the elevator, the doors parting like curtains on a new chapter of her story. This hotel, renowned for its wedding celebrations, offered a daily parade of joy. "Congratulations on your wedding day!" became my frequent and heartfelt greeting. I said it more than a dozen times, each infused with genuine well-wishes for the newlyweds.

There is no story of success without struggle, perfectly declared by Frederick Douglass, "If there is no struggle, there is no progress," as featured by the Black Past Organization in their section about African American history (BlackPast 2007).

OUR FAMILY STRUGGLES

During our first week living in our new home on Long Island, my husband received a call from my brother-in-law, Tony, who lived in Santo Domingo with his family. He gave us the most impactful news we had heard in years.

"Hi there, mi manito (which means little brother in Spanish). We miss you so much here. How is it going, guys?" Tony said.

"All has been great so far. There's a lot to learn, and it gets lonely sometimes. Missing you all too," my husband said.

"Listen, I am not sure if Mom and Dad told you, but last week, I had an episode coming back from a triathlon in Punta Cana. I was in terrible pain and went to the ER. They did an operation since they thought it was my appendix."

His voice suddenly turned grim. "Unfortunately, I don't know where to start…" He cleared his throat and made a long pause.

"What's happening? Are you okay?" My husband changed the phone from one ear to another, closer to me, and held onto my hand.

"Well… when they opened for the appendix operation, they found cancer in some of the organs. We know now where it is located. It's in my colon, and it's spreading," Tony said.

I immediately thought about his wife and two boys the same ages as our kids and felt as if a hole in my stomach had opened. No words could describe the emotions we felt then, the conversations that ensued, and the tears we shed.

We were devastated. My husband's face turned somber and pale.

How is this happening to them? We just moved to US so far away from him and the family. One of our biggest fears became a reality: not being there if something bad happened.

"I just can't believe it, Tony, and I am so sorry this is happening, especially now that I'm away," my husband said.

"This is life, my brother," Tony concluded.

"You will conquer this. Stay positive, and we will support you and the family all the way."

Struggling to think straight, we were in shock, and denial got a hold on us. We shared the news with Ivan and Isabella, who were deeply saddened and could hardly believe it was happening. Distance complicated our challenge of facing a struggle like never before. Instinctively, as a family, we joined hands and said a prayer, seeking strength and hoping for Tony's return to health.

We pressed on, fully aware our decision carried risks. The struggle— very much real—only served to strengthen our family bond.

What else gets in the way if we realize getting out of your comfort zone is important and crucial to your growth? These choices are conditioned most of the time by an element that is always present in our lives and decisions: fear.

As our journey in New York as a family continued, we were not expecting the challenges we would face next.

CHAPTER 4

THE SHOWSTOPPER: FEAR AND HOW IT CAN HOLD YOU BACK

"Everything you've ever wanted is sitting on the other side of fear."
—GEORGE ADDAIR

Many things could stop you from disrupting the status quo, but they all come down to fear.

Fear is a reason for alarm, a sensation that we are in danger, and this precludes us from jumping into situations of uncertainty and revive this sentiment of not being in control. According to the National Institute for Mental Health, based on diagnostic interview data from National Comorbidity Survey Replication among US adults aged eighteen or older, an estimated 12.5 percent of US adults experience specific phobia at some time (National Institute of Mental Health 2023).

To leap out of our lanes, learning to identify the different types of fear and how to manage them is essential. It's not about becoming a fearless person. It is about better understanding your sources of fear, having the courage to confront it, and working to overcome it. Let's explore the most common I hear while mentoring rising leaders or college students, coaching executives, and teams.

FEAR OF TRYING SOMETHING NEW

My son, Ivan, had just turned fifteen when we moved to New York, an upcoming junior in high school. Before coming to the US, he had already applied for an internship through Pace University. He got accepted into the program and was then assigned to a non-profit organization to help with marketing, tech platforms, and digital communications. The internship started the Monday after we arrived in New York City.

He came into our room and said, "Mom, Dad, I've got the address I must report to on Monday, and it's in the city. I googled it, and I need to take a train to Penn Station and then a subway to get there."

I realized my fifteen-year-old, new to this system and this country, had to go to work every day and commute an hour and a half into New York City. Commuting on the LIRR (Long Island Rail Road) and then taking the subway into the city took me a while to understand. I got lost several times between train stops, ending up in Brooklyn instead of getting to Manhattan through Penn Station.

I asked my husband, "Can you take him and ensure he knows his way back? Also, please give him any details to take care of and always be aware of his surroundings." The Latina mom in me made her appearance.

My husband said, "Ivan, I will show you once, then you must go on your own and return."

"Thanks, Dad! I will learn if you show me," said Ivan.

As I reflect on what happened, we reaffirmed to him that he had the courage inside him to do something new and learn through this experience to get to where he needed to go and be independent. In this city, he would have to, and his sister also had to learn and succeed in this new environment. My heart as a mother told me, You are leaving him alone in a big city with many dangers. *Am I crazy, or am I doing the right thing?*

I just had to let him grow up and do it alone. The city of the concrete jungle where dreams are made of—as Alicia Keys and Jay Z describe in their song "Empire State of Mind"—can be too big and overwhelming sometimes, yet it's a perfect place for growth just because you must. There is no other way, or the city can crush you.

This reminds me of a phrase I love and is hanging at home, "Life doesn't have to be perfect to be wonderful."

I had to go to a meeting that day near the city, and as I looked through the office windows on the thirty-eighth floor, I could see that billion-dollar Manhattan skyline clearly, especially on a sunny summer day. That Tuesday morning, I thought, *Am I being the best mom in the world or the worst mom in the world?*

Talking about it with one of my colleagues that morning, he said, "You are raising a courageous young man. Many will not let them go alone to the city, and some Long Islanders don't even want to go either." I felt deep inside—with that mom gut feeling—he would be okay and it would be good for him.

Doing something new is terrifying sometimes, but after you have gone through it and start acting, you learn, get stronger, and grow. The fear levels diminish with time and practice, getting to mastery.

After three months of work, he got an extension of the contract, with a letter of recommendation from the executive director for his college application. Seeing him growing up, conquering something new, and being independent is just great. Until this day, he knows the subway system better than we do!

Doing this internship, learning, having the experience, and thinking about his long-term goal showed his passion. It takes grit and courage to go through this process, and we will see how important this is in your journey as a leaper.

In our Latino culture, we say, "Te tiras al agua de cabeza y sales nadando…" which translates, "We jump in the water, and we learn how to swim."

FEAR OF NAVIGATING THROUGH UNCERTAINTY

Being on an unconventional or completely new path can be stressful and unsettling.

Many elements could go wrong, generating a feeling of giving up control and introducing too many variables in the equation to solve, and that's where "uncertainty" can hit you. Our first six months flew by so fast, and we knew it would be hard as we thought constantly about my brother-in-law's situation and the family. We agreed to fly back to Santo Domingo for the Thanksgiving holiday and share a beautiful moment with the entire family at Tony's house.

He underwent treatment but still battled pain, leading to another surgery and the impending start of chemotherapy. Our family's faith has been our anchor, a lighthouse in the stormy seas in difficult times. Faith has been the bedrock of our family, a constant source of strength through the most challenging times. Your support circle and this connection, this faith, sustains and guides you when paths grow steep. Gratitude filled me with joy from that trip.

The following year, our kids returned to Santo Domingo for summer vacations, and they came back to New York with a somber expression after seeing my brother-in-law.

Isabella said, "Mom, I don't like what I see. He is in too much pain." They were both sad about it, and we continued to pray together.

Tony started new rounds of chemotherapy and showing signs of being stable and progressing. This was good news to treasure. Meanwhile, my in-laws visited us for a week, and we took them to St. Patrick's church in NYC to light a candle and go to mass. Their desire to see Ground Zero led us there next, and we saw the reflective pools that stand where the towers once did, with water endlessly cascading into the vast, dark void below. Together, we stood at the South Tower site, feeling that emptiness, a known sentiment to all who stand before this hallowed ground.

Once we finished, we decided to have lunch in Eataly. Afterward, we started walking to the Oculus Central atrium when my husband suddenly received a call from Tony's wife. He had a heart attack, and they rushed him to the hospital where they revived him, though still not in good condition.

My husband exclaimed in Spanish, "Oh no, Dios mio!"

Her rapid speech and the nervous tremor in her voice conveyed urgency. "I think you should all come to DR. This is not looking good."

I looked at Ivan and Isabella, tears running from our eyes and our faces confused. We started to pray.

My in-laws were devastated and hugged each other, and my mother-in-law cried inconsolably.

We rushed to our vehicle and started heading out of the city through the midtown tunnel to return to Long Island. My sister-in-law, the youngest of the three siblings, called my mobile phone. "Mirna, they are reviving him... Mirna, he is gone."

I stayed put and contained myself the entire ride. I had to think fast to avoid hurting my in-laws and my husband driving the car. He later confided he knew something didn't feel good from the call.

After arriving home, I told my husband and kids about the news. We hugged and cried together, knowing we quickly had to pack. We decided to wait to tell my in-laws until we got to Santo Domingo to avoid a worse situation.

After packing, we headed to the airport around 8:00 p.m. to find the first flight. We told my in-laws of his delicate condition, and after getting to DR, my sister-in-law let them know personally.

I talked to myself while on the plane, "Is it over?" And I realized right after, "Yes, it's over." Our worst fear had become a reality, and to this day, we miss him dearly.

Fast forward to the following year, the night of my award ceremony as the Hispanic Businesswoman of the Year of the Long Island Hispanic Association, I dedicated the award in his honor in my acceptance speech.

Uncertainty is like a wild card in our lives that shows up to remind us we are not in control, yet that shouldn't preclude us from having dreams and betting on ourselves.

Setbacks will come. They are part of life no matter which point you are. They will give you the strength to pause, recalibrate, start over if needed, and keep moving forward.

FEAR OF FAILURE

According to the Forbes Advisor article, "Small Business Statistics of 2023," more than one million small businesses were created, from which 20 percent in the US will fail within the first year and 50 percent in the fifth year (Main 2022).

And many do it anyway.

Considering you are an entrepreneur, why not think you will end up in the 80 percent that do survive that first year instead? Still, the risk will keep you awake at night and freeze you like an ice cube.

Moving with my family to the US posed so many risks. We wondered, *Will we fit in or be able to thrive being ourselves? Being responsible for a profit and loss at my new job tenfold the budget I had managed before, will I succeed?* These were all questions around my fear of failure. Since we moved, we've been living in a town right in the center of Long Island. It's pretty much a suburbia with wide streets, spacious houses, and parks—very different from the city with the Long Islanders' accent, the lack of concrete, and tall buildings, and feeling like a magician if you find a restaurant open after 10:00 p.m. on Sundays.

We chose this town for its top-ranked school district and multicultural community. Predominantly white-Caucasian, the area boasts a significant Jewish population comprising over 40 percent, with Asians making up another 40 percent. Latinos, however, were a rarity, hardly numbering enough to count on both hands, and Spanish-speakers were almost non-existent. This posed a challenge, especially when we arrived in the US. Immigration was a contentious issue at the forefront of a presidential campaign, among other topics on American-made and even campaigns with a call for "immigrants go home."

It reminded me of a conversation I had with one of our friends from Santo Domingo saying to us back in 2016, like many others, "Why are you going to the US when this is the worst time for immigrants and the political climate? You have a great life here."

To bring change into your life, despite the circumstances and the fear of failure, you must understand the why and have this clear.

What is the purpose? What are you gaining from this leap?

It's an *ikigai* moment where our purpose pushes us forward to go through the inconveniences and strive to sort them out and fulfill our dreams. The secret of a long and happy life centers around a person's true purpose, as explained in the article by Renée Onque. It points to Héctor García and Francesc Miralles, authors of *Ikigai: The Japanese Secret to a Long and Happy Life*, who interviewed elderly residents of Okinawa, Japan, the area with the highest concentration of centenaries (Onque 2023).

We had our ikigai clear. We wanted to ensure we did not stay in the arms of complacency and pass up an opportunity just from fear of change, doing something new, or failing to adapt to a new experience or environment. Most importantly, our kids wanted to study abroad in US colleges and had big dreams, and we wanted to get them closer to and open those doors for them. I also had a great opportunity to manage a nationwide product portfolio for the fourth US cable company in the country in the middle of preparing to launch its IPO. How many times would I have the opportunity to experience that?

Should I say, "I'll pass?" Absolutely not.

Knowing your "why" won't necessarily get rid of the fear of failure, but it will give you a reason for going through it. When you know your why, you can also be strategic about approaching your goal, setting yourself up for success. My career journey and personal family story have been more than a fulfilling experience and a reaffirmation that when we leap out of our lane, we can overcome obstacles and have even greater success.

As Oprah Winfrey clearly describes in her heartfelt speech to students at the 2013 Harvard Commencement address about fear of failure,

> "This is what I want to share. It doesn't matter how far you might rise. At some point you are bound to stumble because if you're constantly doing what we do, raising the bar. If you're constantly pushing yourself higher, higher the law of averages, not to mention the Myth of Icarus, predicts that you will at some point fall. And when you do I want you to know this, remember this: there is no such thing as failure. Failure is just life trying to move us in another direction" (Winfrey 2013).

You also must acknowledge that when you are pushing yourself for the next level or in a lateral move to leap out, you will experience setbacks. But it is how you rise from them that gives you the strength to manage change and grow tremendously.

Be intentional with your journey. You must find your "why" and take advantage of any headwind that comes your way as an opportunity to pivot or get stronger.

While working for multinational companies, relocating to another country emerged as a potential future move. Recognizing this, we made sacrifices, not traveling for several years to ensure our children attended bilingual schools. This planning paid dividends when the possibility of moving became a reality. Our children were fully bilingual, prepared, and ready to embrace school life in the US.

We will further discuss the benefits of planning before you take a leap and being strategic as part of your playbook in part three.

FEAR OF OTHERS' PERCEPTIONS AND EXCLUSION

I recall the first meeting with one of the school officials. He laid it out clearly about being a school of excellence and how they didn't even rank their students as they were all high achievers. What a jarring moment.

I looked him directly and said, "Our kids are in academic excellence in their former school, and they followed a high-standards English curriculum throughout all their school years. You can see this in their letters of recommendation and transcript."

His expression turned more amicable, and he started to provide more information about the school and the enrollment process.

> Perceptions and beliefs of others can make you
> feel undermined, but that is all they are.

I recall a story from one data analyst who reported to my organization. She served in the United States Air Force, coming from a family with a strong military background. Facing skepticism from her cousins as she prepared for training, she proved that not only could a woman excel in the military, but she too possessed what it takes. To this day, she encounters raised eyebrows from those who remark she doesn't fit the mold of a typical military member. Such comments lead her to ask,

"What does 'typical' even mean?" These moments present a prime opportunity to challenge perceptions and enlighten the curious.

On your side, you always have the true story, and you must drive your narrative with facts while being humble and assertive. Also, in the end, this is more their problem to solve than your problem.

Don't let this drive you away from your objective.

Going back to the conversation with that school administrator: Our kids were stressed out, and my son said, "Mom, I'm going to have to compete with other kids who have been studying the SAT already for years, and I could be at a disadvantage here. They have more advanced placement classes than I even had access to."

I looked both kids in their eyes and said, "It is better to challenge yourself to high standards to be the best version of yourself rather than staying where you feel comfortable. Look at us; here we are."

Our kids had to go through many challenges, like that awkward moment you see in movies, such as sitting alone or being mocked in the cafeteria and not being invited to a pizza party or a sports club gathering since they were different for some of them.

Isabella started middle school, and the adaptation challenge took us by storm. Questions such as "You're Mexican, right? Did you cross the border to get here?" were not uncommon, reflecting how media and political rhetoric had shaped some people's views, often equating immigration with illegality. Such misconceptions should have accounted for the diverse ways many of us take, and such courage is commendable, but being mislabeled is hard.

Nevertheless, they found many welcoming people in the school governance, like the assistant principal, originally from the

Dominican Republic, respecting and caring for all the faculty and students, who were open to embracing diversity and getting to know them better.

Our kids managed to succeed not only academically but also from a social perspective, making amazing new friends and both graduating with high honors. Isabella transformed this situation into a movement, creating a club to address diversity and inclusion with a visible impact in students and activities that supported their mission to learn about other cultures. She also managed to have her school play "merengue" and "salsa" in their morning address during Diversity week.

Most importantly, they got through it, coming off stronger, transforming a situation of adversity in their favor, and being better equipped to handle these situations if presented in the future. Listening, observing, knowing your loved ones, providing support, and letting them find their way out is essential. They will find their own way out. In our case, we were raised with those values, we urged them to jump into situations of change and learn something new, and we also challenged them to confront change. Even if you are privileged and have the means, this concept still applies.

Stay humble, stay hungry, and just do it!

FEAR OF FINANCIAL STRUGGLE

You are considering launching yourself into a different path, career, or new challenge. In that case, there is always the uncertainty of how this will affect you personally or your immediate family, and this is even more delicate if you have kids. It can be unsettling. Nevertheless, creating a plan and evaluating the initial risks is doable. In addition to this planning, we must define a contingency plan for what's expected during a transition period.

Consider Lily, an entrepreneur who has her own coaching practice and used to work for a cable company for many years. She decided to launch her practice, find clients, and start her coaching business while working full-time. She planned how to achieve it and even moved with her husband to another state with lower living costs to make the transition more attainable and have a better quality of life.

Planning during this period can help if a sudden change comes our way, such as losing our jobs or moving to another place that implies a change of jobs.

If you manage to plan, it makes it more controllable. You define the scenarios you are willing to accept, and always have a plan B you can fall back on if things get off track. It's important to consider the scenarios carefully and the "what ifs" before jumping into a new challenge or situation.

Consider Ana, another entrepreneur in the beauty business whose establishment I visited while in Florida for a quinceañera event. She had been working in a hair salon for fifteen years and wanted to be independent, but she feared the financial struggle while having a family. Issues at work had arrived with new management, and she lost her job. At that moment, she picked herself up and, with some savings, established her beauty salon, and she has been thriving ever since even when an unplanned situation happened.

I found an interesting approach in an article from BetterUp about financial stress, stating that it can cause symptoms similar to anxiety and can be as severe as post-traumatic stress disorder (PTSD) when you feel you cannot get ahead of the bills no matter how hard you work. Allaya Cooks-Campbell asserts, "Financial stress is a state of worry, anxiety, or emotional tension related to money, debt, and upcoming or current expenses. Money is one of the most universal sources of stress" (Cooks-Campbell 2021).

Some of the recommendations to manage financial stress effects include self-awareness and mindfulness as support systems to cope. More so, to avoid financial stress, planning is the key as you navigate the world of incorporating changes in your life. Some recommendations include creating a budget, reducing expenses such as duplicative ones, finding ways to generate extra money, having an emergency fund, starting small, and going easy on yourself not wanting to solve everything at once.

This resonates with our early life as a couple and family as well. Sometimes, if we were not able to solve for the month, we would concentrate on solving the week, if not the hour, if not even the minute. This will give you a sense of improvement and satisfaction that will best position you to problem-solve and face the next challenge.

From early on in our marriage, our faith and beliefs were pivotal in confronting our fears and bonding as a family. Our supportive community includes our brothers and sisters at our local church, and we have been working on couples' and families' counsel for more than nineteen years. We could see how families starting with divisions and deep wounds will emerge stronger and transform their lives. When you participate in activities that give back, you feel whole, which is a blessing for your family.

To move forward with a leaper's mindset, we need to identify and conquer our fears and be prepared with the tools to face them. Our fears can be holding us back, and going through them can be often daunting until we beat them.

Seeking help from a coach or expert is always encouraged, as this can accelerate your process of conquering this milestone, getting unstuck, managing situations of trauma and helping you to move on, and starting your planning to greater growth.

I am rooting for you all the way.

PART 2

THE LEAPER'S PLAYBOOK

CHAPTER 5

THE LEAPER'S PLAYBOOK: EIGHT STRATEGIES TO EMBRACE CHANGE

"He allowed himself to be swayed by his conviction that human beings are not born once and for all on the day their mothers give birth to them, but that life obliges them over and over again to give birth to themselves."

—GABRIEL GARCÍA MÁRQUEZ, *LOVE IN THE TIME OF CHOLERA*

TAKING THE LEAP AND A NON-TRADITIONAL PATH

During the second half of 2018, my husband also found a new job in a big tech consulting company. He started flying back and forth to Boston weekly during his first assignment. The winter played a cruel card with more than five nor'easters, blizzards, and storms I've seen in the last seven years. I learned how to shovel snow and saw a seven-foot-tall pile of snow on the side of the streets formed by the plows. The latest storm brought so much snow that our vehicles were covered completely, and I learned the hard way why it is better to leave the windshield wipers up to make it easier to scrape the snow from your car's windshield.

One day, while sitting in my office in Long Island, I felt my hands could turn blue—despite the heater—if I clutched the hot tea mug I held. My leading of the transformation process immersed me in the following steps while laying the groundwork for the next year's plan.

I had recently reshuffled some of the leaders within my team into different areas based on their skills and potential. Like Sarah, a leader whom I had identified as high-potential and who had been helping me craft some of the turnaround strategies. She was one of the leaders whose responsibilities I shifted within the team.

"Mirna, I can't do it!" She spatted this out while entering my office.

"Do what, Sarah?" I replied.

"I can't do the role you asked me to do. Agh! I've always worked with medium-enterprise segments, and I can't do this small business segment job you ask me to take. I don't want to spend my life working non-stop, and not everyone wants to be you!"

I gave her a look to calm down. "Sarah, who told you to leave all you have learned behind and lose your family? I want to tell you something: You are a high achiever and high potential. This is why you must take this opportunity and embrace it. It will be hard at the beginning, but you will apply all the principles and knowledge you have to this new segment. I got your back. Sarah, this is mutually beneficial for you and the company."

"I am appreciative of that, Mirna. I just don't see it."

Seeing through the noise of learning something did not make it click for her, having to throw herself into the unchartered waters. The status quo could be winning the battle. On the contrary, I envisioned something for her much bigger. I usually identify several high potentials and challenge them to prepare for a more significant role in the future.

The way to move forward is to pave the way for others. They will then push you forward, and you will have a succession plan for the next opportunity.

I explained the good behind the decision. "Sarah, you are not seeing it now, but this new segment represents 85 percent of our revenues, and it's a critical part of our business." Her eyes were watery as she rubbed her forehead, absorbing and internalizing my words.

"I don't want to work long hours. Not everyone wants the same things." Her voice cut at the end of the sentence.

"You don't have to. It is a personal decision to come here and learn all these new things, a new culture. You don't have to run at the same pace or do exactly as I do. Listen, there will come a time when learning this new area and accepting the challenge will accelerate your career and exposure. You will get involved in taking more challenging decisions with a much larger impact on the company, and that will help you grow." This move created in her a vision of what she would become and put her on a path to leap out and adopt the leaper's mindset.

Fast forward several years, she is now vice president of marketing and managing a larger team. She is also thriving with her family with two gorgeous boys, helping them grow up while rocking it on the marketing team. As she leaped out, the lateral move helped her learn new skills she applied in the next challenge.

THE LEAPER'S MINDSET

*Being a leaper is a mindset, a way of living that
will open new doors and possibilities for you as
you embrace change as a catalyst for growth.*

I'm doing it again by writing this book, *Leap Out of Your Lane*, becoming an author, and designing a playbook to help others succeed as I did. Up to this point, we have seen the foundations needed to shape the leaper's mindset and why you need this in your life now to futureproof yourself as you navigate and seek changes. Leapers embody true authentic leadership. They are proactive, confident, adaptable to work, manage to have intentionality by being strategic, plan ahead to mitigate risks, and bring teams together through empathy.

As I embarked on this new journey of being an author, I started taking steps early to plan accordingly, including making an inventory of people whom I would describe as "leapers" I wanted to interview for this book.

One of the first leapers who came to mind is my dear friend Stephanie Nuesi, whom I learned from through the LinkedIn community. As I described briefly in the introduction of the book, her path has been a non-traditional one, going from not knowing English at all and living in a low-income town in the Dominican Republic without even enough means to have food on her table, to learning English in record time, graduating from Baruch College in New York, landing a job in big tech at Google, and also being the founder and CEO of Max Up in just six to seven years. She has more than 250,000 followers and over 150 million views on LinkedIn.

I interviewed Stephanie around springtime, at a time where she recently moved to California working at her dream job at a Fortune 100 big tech, had already finished building a house in the Dominican Republic for her parents, helped them retire, and launched her coaching practice, including an e-learning course. Helping to navigate clients' careers, position themselves, and build the brand they want is the purpose she has with her company the Max Up.

She greeted me with a big smile that is almost contagious, her bright eyes bursting with excitement, and we started the conversation. "I wanted to create a legacy while I'm alive," Stephanie said. I thought, *She is only twenty-four...* I looked at her so young. "I feel like one of the stigmas in society is that you must be a certain age to do something or have specific experience, which is not necessarily the case. I want to show people that, no matter what age you are or where you come from, it's still possible for you to do impressive things."

"Stephanie, I know many people can get inspired by you. We have both seen what the power of education can do. I also love and feel myself identified with the story of your parents and how you show gratitude for all they did for you and how your mom encouraged you not to give up." Her mom worked as an electrician with no high school diploma, and she did it even in the extreme heat situations under the Caribbean sun, while her dad lived in New York.

"I had just one dream to make my parents' sacrifices worth it, and it became a reality after all the rejections. I applied to more than eighty colleges in the US and got rejected from all of them because I didn't know English. And a year later, after studying English at a public library—we couldn't afford to pay for private classes—I got accepted to Baruch in NYC."

Stephanie continued her story, "That's when the real challenge started. I was doing two jobs while going to school and doing internships while doing all these different things, and I started my business, Max Up, when I was still in school. I wanted to do all these things simultaneously, so I could say I built a legacy by the time I graduated from college, and it became a reality."

CHALLENGES, FAILURES, AND REJECTIONS

Stephanie graduated from college with excellent grades, despite learning English in a short period of time. She is the first in her my family to graduate from college in the US, the first to speak English, and the first to land a job in corporate America and launch her own business.

I could see the grit and the courage in her, as well as the gratitude for the opportunities she took and the challenges she faced, all which made her stronger.

"What kept you going, Stephanie, and how did you overcome those challenges?" I asked.

She reflected on these accomplishments, and her big brown eyes opened wider as she talked. "There are many different firsts to hold there, and people don't see it or understand the responsibilities. Your family is counting on you, and you have an entire country behind where you are opening so many doors for others you don't even realize. And that's what kept me going to where I am now. I like to say the rejections I faced in life, the failures, the challenges, all of them built me up to the success I have now.

"Let me start with the first one, which is English. I used to feel ashamed of my accent. I used to feel like I was not good enough. I broke this challenge by staying true to myself and not forgetting where I come from. These are the values my mom instilled in me very early on. I learned from the example from my mom, as she came here to the US to ensure I could go to school."

Both of her parents were early risers and worked hard to support her. Her mom left everything she knew at the age of fifty to start working in a country with a different language, waking up at 3:00 a.m. every day without complaining. How could Stephanie complain? "I always thought about how I could give up. That was one of the major factors that kept me going and motivated me even through all the rejections," she said.

"I remember I already had Max Up, and even before, I was already helping people with their résumés, cover letters, interviews... And when people messaged me, 'Oh, Stephanie, you changed my life,' or, 'Stephanie, I got the job because of your help,' that was enough motivation to keep going even when I got all those rejections from colleges or from corporate jobs I wanted. I just kept going."

To Stephanie, it all paid off, and she got emotional in our call and remembered how much she had to go through. Her message was, "Failures and rejections are redirection, and so sometimes I would get rejected from certain opportunities, but then a better opportunity would come into my life."

This experience in this interview with Stephanie reminded me of a quote I read in the book *UNLIMITED: The Seventeen Proven Laws for Success in a Workplace Not Designed for You*, by Eugina Jordan, an author and CMO of a telecommunications organization: "Believe in your value and the importance of it despite where you come from" (Jordan 2023, 94).

As you leap out, failures and rejections are ways of redirecting you to something much more prosperous and fruitful in your life.

As my family adapted to the first year and had to go through loss and grief, we grew stronger from those moments of hardship. We also started to see the wins in our lives with my promotion to senior vice president after the first year. I have great achievements, and I am already managing a $1.4 billion product portfolio. That year, I also learned how to launch an initial public offering (IPO), building the transferrable skills that contributed to my growth as an executive in corporate America.

I took on the challenge of spearheading a special project to launch an entirely new business unit for the company, building it from the ground up, and diving into this new venture within the same organization. This thrilling project added to my existing duties, and I later had the opportunity to hand over leadership to new talents who continued with the product's launch.

That second year, not all of it was rosy and good news. The rhetoric around immigrants going home continued, and the impact of it as a family was hard felt. The year 2018 was turbocharged with allegations that created division in how people felt about us and questions we got all the time. As an executive, I experienced hate firsthand in several meetings. It was then a decision to sponsor our families and start the process of adjustment of status as permanent residents. This came as a shock for our family and friends back in Santo Domingo. We were staying in the USA permanently and following the path to becoming citizens.

During our third year living in NYC, Ivan graduated high school with high honors, achieved an impressive SAT score, and was accepted to his dream school, NYU Stern School of Business—a milestone moment. I was in the middle of a meeting and received a call. It was my husband and my son screaming out of his lungs, "I got in!" I left everything and started screaming with happiness and joy! I think everyone understood this was a college decision, as I was ecstatic.

Also, our daughter Isabella was thriving in school, getting high honors, and finding new friends who cared for her and were also high achievers. She had yet to decide what she wanted to do and which college to attend.

We like the life and place we now call home. We like to be part of the community and serve, still understanding that our tropical island and roots will always be in our hearts. One of the managers on my team made us a present for the holidays that year, a painting of the US with a red heart over New York and a white dotted line that extends to the same red heart over Dominican Republic. This person was Sarah, and it was a sign of connection and unity. There is always a guiding light, and God constantly shapes us to build ourselves stronger to keep thriving.

THE LEAPER'S PLAYBOOK

Learning from these leaper's stories, my career, and personal journey; and interviewing high-achieving individuals, executives, entrepreneurs, and founders, I see a typical pattern in how people who leap out of their lanes successfully do it. This is how I have experienced our leaper tribe behave and the mindset we carry forward in our lives.

Consider Jessica Alba, who, from being a successful and renowned actress, in 2015 leapt out into becoming an entrepreneur and launching a $550 million business, despite the naysayers who thought she wouldn't make it, as she expressed in a CNBC interview (Scipioni 2022). She started The Honest Company, inspired by her first-born child. It offers consumer goods known for its commitment to ethical and sustainable products, representing a significant shift from Alba's acting career, highlighting her business savvy and adaptability becoming a leaper herself.

I met Jessica at the launch event of her new home renovations show at the chief headquarters in NYC, where she shared with the audience her story of humble beginnings and the company launch inspired by her immigrant parents, who were also entrepreneurs. And now, she has created an empire and continues to thrive.

I want to share a different story that impacted my life when I first saw a YouTube video about it some years ago, and I share it in team-building activities or planning sessions.

The story of the Panyee Football Club, reported by Euronews in their 2023 article, takes us to the village of Koh Panyee, located on the coast of Thailand. A group of young boys shared a love for soccer and could not have a place to practice, due to living on a landmass of less than a kilometer in diameter, and most of the houses—or what they call a hut—are built over the water. With such a passion for soccer, these youngsters wanted to play and have a team. They came to the resolution to build their own soccer field on the water (Ward et al. 2023).

The community had such skepticism, and some laughed at their idea. In the article, one of the F.C. Panyee members, Hadi, said, "The first pitch was made from fish cages covered with wooden planks. They made a raft and took leftover pieces of iron and made goalposts." When the community saw they were serious and determined, they started to support the cause, helping them build the first version. Sometimes, they would need to get in the water to look for the ball, and as they play barefoot, they had to be careful with nails on the wooden surface.

They overcame adversity with grit and courage by trying something new for what they cared about and were passionate about. They got the community engaged, and they became their cheerleaders along their path of becoming champions in their regions for several years. Having scarce resources even to buy proper shoes, they would practice barefoot, which gave them special skills as well as playing over the water with the instability and bouncing of the ball. They built strength through these challenging conditions to play even under the pouring rain. Nowadays, this community receives more than three thousand visitors a day, bringing prosperity to this area and putting them on the map where their inhabitants have additional means to improve their lives and community.

These are leapers, game-changers who don't accept no for an answer and redirect their focus to what will solve the problem or get them to meet their goal. Their vision was clear, with a community rooting and supporting them.

The leaper's playbook, by design, uses the foundational elements we have seen so far and will take you through the step-by-step on what shapes a leaper and how you can redirect and be more equipped for dealing with change.

As a product executive and marketer, I'll show you the roadmap. We will dive deep into the eight strategies in this playbook to help you successfully incorporate change into your lifestyle and manage it to work for you and not against you. The first four strategies are foundational before going through a leap. In part three, we will explore the other four that will help you build your blueprint. This will serve as your toolkit to help you leap out of your lane and make change be your currency

Eight Strategies to Embrace Change

1) Self-awareness
Knowing yourself better, identifying your superpowers and what's holding you back.

2) Being a constant learner
Having a growth mindset and the will to improve.

3) Embrace grit
Having the courage to pursue your passion relentlessly.

4) Build resilience and confidence
Prepare yourself for navigating uncertain moments.

5) Purpose-driven life
Discover your purpose and why to define your path to success.

6) Take action
Plan, measure, and use intentionality to succeed.

7) Change as a lifestyle
Take control of your life by being flexible and adaptable and incorporating change into your everyday life. Drive your life forward and pivot when necessary.

8) Leaper's tribe
Community and support; where you build your tribe and cheerleaders; and paying it forward to live a fulfilling and successful life through changes.

If you boost your mindset and follow this framework, you will create a blueprint to get there, change your life, and achieve the unimaginable.

LEAPER'S PLAYBOOK:
THE EIGHT STRATEGIES TO EMBRACE CHANGE

STRATEGY #1: SELF-AWARENESS AND COMPASSION	STRATEGY #5: A PURPOSE-DRIVEN LIFE
STRATEGY #2: GRIT AND COURAGE: PASSION PIVOT, AND PRESERVANCE	STRATEGY #6: TAKE ACTION AND MOVE FORWARD
STRATEGY #3: BEING A CONSTANT LEARNER: SHIFTING YOUR MINDSET	STRATEGY #7: CHANGE AS YOUR LIFESTYLE
STRATEGY #4: BUILDING RESILIENCE AND SELF-CONFIDENCE	STRATEGY #8: LEAPER'S CHEERLEADERS — DEFINE YOUR TRIBE

Illustration credit: Marigina Eusebio Lithgow | LEAPERS PLAYBOOK credit: Mirna Eusebio Lithgow

Leaper's Tip

You will always find someone who has an opinion on your project or direction in life or naysayers who don't believe in your dreams. Keep moving forward with what you believe to be true, building the plan and foundation for success.
Open your possibilities by exploring this step-by-step guide, as we dive deep in each strategy and start your new "you." We are creating a blueprint together.

CHAPTER 6

STRATEGY #1: SELF-AWARENESS AND COMPASSION

"Knowing others is intelligence; knowing yourself is true wisdom. Mastering others is strength; mastering yourself is true power."

—LAO TZU

SELF-AWARENESS AND INTROSPECTION

The quest for self-awareness has become more essential in a rapidly changing world. Being a constant learner and understanding myself through introspection has become a powerful personal growth and development tool I have leveraged throughout my career.

Tasha Eurich is the author of *Insight: The Surprising Truth About How Others See Us, How We See Ourselves, and Why the Answers Matter More Than We Think*. With her team of researchers, they discovered that while 95 percent of people claim to be self-aware, only 10 to 15 percent fit the criteria.

She says in her Ted Talk, which has more than 4.3 million views:

> There is strong scientific evidence that people who know them-
> selves and how others see them are happier. They make smarter
> decisions. They have better personal and professional relation-
> ships. They raise more mature children. They're smarter, superior
> students who choose better careers. They're more creative, more
> confident, and better communicators (Eurich 2017).

In that same line, we see that introspection is a fascinating process
that allows individuals to delve into the depths of their minds,
exploring the intricate workings of their thoughts, emotions, and
perceptions. Humans possess the unique ability to turn our attention
inward and engage in self-reflection. Through introspection, we can
better understand ourselves, our motivations, and the underlying
factors that shape our behavior, paving the way for personal growth
and self-awareness.

I recall the first time I was exposed to the concepts by my first
manager at Verizon. I worked hard to get a manager position, and
after more than a year of positioning myself for the job, I didn't get
it. One of my colleagues did.

I was furious—visibly upset—and could be seen often talking to my
other colleagues about how unfair this process was. I felt like an
architect, and someone else had cut the ribbon for the building I had
designed with effort. I said those exact words to my manager then. In
a brief meeting, he called to deal with the situation in the all-crystal
conference room—no wonder people call it the fishbowl—and what
he said to me next made me feel even worse. "Mirna, you have to
understand there is a legacy element, and it's her turn, not yours."

Have you ever experienced that moment of lacking fairness and
transparency? You have probably experienced that similar feeling

of not being tenured enough or experienced enough, and it's other people's turn. Hopefully, some of you have not.

It's frustrating. This wasn't the first time, and it wouldn't be the last for me or anyone.

Days later, I got an invite to a meeting with my manager's boss, who used to be my professor in college and referred me for my first internship opportunity in this company. I opened the door to his office, greeted him politely, and proceeded to sit down as he approached the big conference room table inside his office. After he sat at the other end of the conference room, he said, "Mirna, you know I appreciate your work, and you are a great professional. I know you didn't get the promotion, but you must see it as a learning experience, dig deeper, and do some introspection." He encouraged me, suggesting my time to shine was on the horizon, and urged me to persevere.

There you go. I now had this new word in my life: "introspection."

I initially doubted how this would help me.

However, it turned out to be truly beneficial advice, and it remains one of the best I have received over the years.

When you apply introspection to your life, you start to see the opportunities and manage to think better about how to rise above the situation and the noise. To get what you want and to greater success, you must conquer yourself, your limitations, and your perceptions, not others.

My mom also helped me get unstuck in the idea that I didn't get what I deserved and worked so hard for. She told me over the phone, "You can stay in that sad little box you have brought yourself into, or you can fight and get out and open yourself to get better and make this happen."

Short story: I ended up being a great asset to my new boss, and she recommended me for a promotion a year later. I got a job in management that I so much wanted and worked hard for. I focused on proving my value but also looking inside to what led me to not get the promotion in the first place—what I had to do to improve.

Introspection is now part of my daily routine after this experience. I even took a better management job in a different division, since I had two job offers from different leaders who wanted me within the same company.

I didn't have a promotion at first and ended up having a better job than expected.

A pivotal moment in my journey of self-discovery unfolded as I watched a Ted Talk by Dr. Brené Brown, a renowned researcher who delves into the complexities of shame and vulnerability. Her insights illuminated the paradoxical nature of vulnerability, a revelation that resonated with me. Dr. Brown asserts, "I know that vulnerability is the core of shame and fear and our struggle for worthiness, but it appears that it's also the birthplace of joy, of creativity, of belonging, of love" (Brown 2010). This statement sparked a profound understanding of vulnerability's dual role for me.

We gain valuable insights about our strengths, weaknesses, and aspirations through introspection. By examining our thoughts, emotions, and motivations, we can identify behavior patterns, limiting beliefs, and areas where improvement is needed. This self-awareness forms the foundation for initiating positive changes and better understanding ourselves.

YOUR INNER CRITIC: RENOUNCING YOUR ANTI-HEROES

It is no secret to many of my colleagues, friends, and family that, like my daughter Isabella, I have been a true fan of Taylor Swift for years and am part of her "Swifties" tribe. Taylor Swift is an example of a leaper who goes way beyond in all aspects of her life and out of her comfort zone. She leaped out of her lane to establish new paths, business models, and ways to shape the industry completely differently—to her benefit and others. This is managing change and uncertainty and being the catalyst for change.

One of my favorite songs from Taylor is "Anti-hero" from her latest album, *Midnights*. As reported by iHeartMedia, Taylor discloses her sentiment to this song on her Instagram page: "This song really is a real guided tour throughout all the things I tend to hate about myself. We all hate things about ourselves," she said. "So yeah, I like 'Anti-hero' a lot because I think it's really honest" (Gonzalez 2022).

She has shown in a very transparent way her vulnerabilities and way of coping and moving forward. This has not stopped her from being herself, showing up for others, and being a change agent.

Which are your anti-heroes? Are they stopping you from making that change you need and want?

Taylor Swift has undeniably left her mark on the music industry, particularly when advocating for musicians' rights. Her determination to protect artists and their creative works has sparked a wave of change within the industry. Swift's pivotal moment came in 2014 when she removed her entire catalog from the popular music streaming platform Spotify, as a protest to the platform's treatment to artists' work and compensation. This bold move ignited a global conversation about streaming royalties and shed light on practices artists faced in the digital era. She started a movement that prompted other musicians to speak out against inequitable contracts and payment structures, leading to new platforms and models prioritizing fair compensation and transparency for musicians.

Moreover, Taylor Swift's legal battles have brought significant attention to ownership and artistic control issues. In 2019, Swift made headlines when she publicly condemned the sale of her master recordings to a private equity firm without her consent. Her efforts to regain control over her music and promote the importance of ownership have inspired many musicians to reassess their contracts and demand greater control over their artistic endeavors. In turn, record labels and streaming platforms have been pushed to reevaluate their practices, leading to discussions around fairer contracts, more favorable licensing terms, and improved transparency in the music industry (Shonk 2023).

We see here an example of managing change and throwing yourself into the waters of creating meaningful change and winning while you do this, despite your struggles and dealing with your *anti-heroes*. We could go on and on.

Taylor Swift's life journey is a great example of a leaper's journey, going from songwriter to producer to movie director and a marketing genius. She is now declared a billionaire for her efforts, according to Bloomberg estimates (Maruf 2023).

How did I ended up being a "Swiftie"? Taylor's relationship with her mom and how this impacted the bond between me and my daughter drew me to follow the artist. I recall a moment when we flew to Miami, Florida, for our first concert ever in Taylor Swift's *1989* tour at the American Airlines Arena. We planned this for an entire year as Isabella's tenth birthday gift. The loud sound perfectly mixed with a crowd cheering her songs like I'd never seen before. Attendee bracelets that would light up to the beat of the music, dancers' costumes in bright colors, special effects... you name it. All the moms and even dads singing the lyrics of the songs and cheering with their kids struck me the most! That is getting to people's hearts, and it felt different.

SELF-COMPASSION TO HELP YOU MOVE ON

When we are too harsh on ourselves, we can damage our self-esteem, which gets in the way of our improvement and taking on new challenges.

Dr. Kristin Neff, a researcher and professor from the University of Texas at Austin, is a leading expert on self-compassion and has also contributed significant research to understanding the inner critic. Neff's studies suggest the inner critic is rooted in our instinctual self-preservation system, designed to protect us from potential threats and failure. However, when this critical voice becomes overactive, it can hinder personal growth, resilience, and well-being (Neff 2023).

Neff states that responding to our inner critic with self-compassion means treating ourselves with kindness, understanding, and acceptance, just as we would treat a struggling close friend. It involves recognizing that suffering and imperfection are a part of the shared human experience, fostering a sense of common humanity. Lastly, self-compassion requires mindful awareness, where we acknowledge and observe our thoughts and emotions without judgment, allowing us to respond with compassion and care (David 2023).

As a leaper, I've realized that sometimes I'm too harsh with myself when going through all these changes. Then I conclude what I'm doing is not an easy task and even involves, in some cases, starting over from scratch.

Be compassionate first with yourself. Give
yourself some grace. You got this!

Dr. Neff recommends several exercises to cultivate self-compassion and counteract the inner critic. One effective exercise is the "self-compassion break." (You can find more information about this and other exercises at www.Self-Compassion.org.) This practice involves three simple steps:

1) We acknowledge our pain or suffering by recognizing and validating our emotions.
2) We remind ourselves that we are not alone in our struggles, recognizing that suffering is a part of the human experience.
3) Lastly, we offer ourselves kind and compassionate words of comfort, such as, "May I be kind to myself," or, "May I give myself the love and understanding I need." This exercise helps shift our self-talk from self-criticism to self-compassion.

Another valuable exercise is the "self-compassionate letter." In this exercise, we write a letter to ourselves, addressing the pain, challenges, or mistakes we are currently experiencing. We approach ourselves with kindness, understanding, and support, offering compassion and encouragement. This exercise allows us to practice self-kindness and develop a nurturing internal dialogue (David 2023).

Incorporating these self-compassion exercises into our daily lives can weaken our inner critic's grip and cultivate a more compassionate and accepting relationship with ourselves.

Through self-kindness, recognition of common humanity, and mindfulness, we can nourish our well-being, foster personal growth, and develop a resilient and self-compassionate mindset.

As we continue our journey together, let's take a deeper dive on the following tool: grit and courage.

Leaper's Tip

Let's reflect on this chapter.
Ask yourself, where am I right now?
Am I being too harsh on others and primarily on myself?
Is this hindering my ability to take on new challenges or taking that leap to greater success?
Which actions can I take from this chapter to incorporate in my life right now?

CHAPTER 7

STRATEGY #2: GRIT AND COURAGE: PASSION, PIVOT, AND PERSEVERANCE

"Grit is passion and perseverance for long-term goals. Grit is having stamina. Grit is sticking with your future, day-in, day-out, not for a week, or a month but for years and working really hard to make that future a reality."

—ANGELA LEE DUCKWORTH

DISCOVERING GRIT TO PERSEVERE AND ACHIEVE YOUR GOAL

As we continue exploring the steps to greater success and growth, let's deep dive into two concepts I appreciate and have helped tremendously along my career journey: grit and courage.

I found one of the best definitions of grit through an Angela Duckworth Ted Talk with more than thirteen million views on YouTube, and I included it at the beginning of this chapter. In her late twenties, Angela left a demanding job as a management consultant at McKinsey & Company to teach math in public schools in San

Francisco, Philadelphia, and New York. After five years of teaching seventh graders, she returned to grad school to complete her PhD in psychology at the University of Pennsylvania. In this Ted Talk, she walked the audience through her study of what makes West Point cadets, spelling bee participants, teachers in complex and under-represented school districts, and sales representatives in companies more successful than others (Duckworth 2023).

She challenged that IQ is the measure of success, and instead, what research has discovered is the one thing all these high performers have from these distinctive groups: grit. She goes deeper into this concept and research, as she explains in her book, *Grit: Passion and Perseverance*. To prove the motivations underlying grit, she recruited sixteen thousand American adults and asked them to complete a grit scale, a test that will tell how gritty they are. She also concluded through the study results that gritty people are more motivated to seek a meaningful, other-centered life, and the high scores on purpose also correlated with the scores on the grit scale (Duckworth 2023).

Grit and courage for what you believe is your passion will help you organize your life to the changes needed to achieve your goal. It will keep you focused, adapt, and pivot if needed despite the headwinds that could come your way. This is not just some pretty phrase to put together. As you can see, this is backed by science.

FINDING THE COURAGE TO PIVOT

During sophomore year in high school, my son started his college application process and had to navigate taking multiple advanced placement (AP) classes. We had no idea of the complexity of the college process in the US and that you must start your SAT/ACT classes in your early years in high school. Some students even start in middle school.

My son, a soccer fan, aspired to join the school's varsity team that year but faced stiff competition. Instead, he made it to the school varsity football team and used that as a springboard to connect with new friends.

Still, he would get home and say, "Mom, it's hard to break circles created for a long time, and I'm unable to get in." For him, this is important, and he has always been an overachiever at school and a social kid. I told him, "You will find a way into amazing friends. You have it in you, and you know how to be a great friend too. They will notice. You'll see."

One day, it happened.

Back in the Dominican Republic, he took an extra-curricular activity, musical production, and DJing. To our surprise, this hobby helped him through his senior year, as he used this passion to become the official DJ of his school and his prom, being invited to every party, making lots of friends, and generating some extra money.

The night of the school homecoming party came in with a big turnout. As a mom of a senior, I served on the activities committee. Part of our responsibilities involved selling the tickets and other items at the front desk for the prom funds.

One of the assistant principals introduced himself and said, "You have an amazing and caring kid." He did his research and got all the kids in the room and teachers dancing all night with terrific music.

Later that night, the principal approached me and said, "Are you Ivan's mom?"

"Yes. Nice to see you, Mrs. Thompson," I said, still puzzled by her approach and wondering what was going on.

She said, "I've been the principal of this school for many years, and I have to be honest. I've never seen so many students dancing for a while… and they were all dancing. This is a miracle!"

That day marked a significant turning point in his senior year. He used his talent to find a way to get through an obstacle, persevere, and achieve what he wanted. All this has a purpose in his life, to show him he could thrive in any environment and pivot if he was determined to change the status quo. Fast forward to the end of the year, Ivan graduated high school with high grades and honors, got a high score on his SAT, navigated through the college application process—no comments, such a complicated and competitive process—and got into his dream school, NYU Stern School of Business.

In life, as in business, we need to be flexible enough to change our approach when needed and pivot. If something is not working or not good enough for our purposes and goals, we sometimes have to detach from our original strategy and change to a new one. Grit can be applied in our everyday life as in our professional life as leaders. Having the courage to change the course or adapting to new situations to persevere will take us farther.

FIND INNER STRENGTH TO ACHIEVE YOUR GOALS

My younger sister, Marigina, also inspired me to write this book. She is such a creative mind and always had an appreciation and love for art at a young age like no one I've ever seen. When I started college and got into one of the most important business schools in the Dominican Republic for my undergraduate in marketing, my parents wanted her to follow in my steps and do the same. She struggled with the idea since she wanted to study communications and advertising, and my dad opposed it since he didn't see it as a real career at the time.

I admire my sister's courage. One day, after her first year in college studying marketing—we attended the same school—she stopped me in one of the hallways and said, "Mirna, I can't do this anymore. I don't want to study marketing!" I understood her reasoning and told her to talk to dad and that I would support her even if we had to pay for it together.

She said later to my dad, "Dad, I'm dropping out of marketing, and I got accepted to my dream school to study communications and arts. I know it is not what you wanted, but this is what I want, and I'm good at it and want to do this for the rest of my life." Boom, she dropped it.

Did my dad enjoy the news? Not that much, but he let it go. After all these years, she is now a successful designer and founder of her own licensing company.

I wanted to include her story as I know college-bound high schoolers have doubts about what to do and don't have it all figured out yet, and I want you to know it is okay. What you want to do is more important, and you will apply your knowledge in whichever area you develop. If not, you can always pivot. To the parents, if your kids are determined and know what they want in life, count this as a blessing and support them.

After my son got into college, the COVID-19 pandemic hit and brought us back together to work and study from home like the rest of the world. It was a tough time, and we didn't even have the security of seeing our families back in the Dominican Republic again. When things started to open up again around 2021, we decided one day to go back to an operation that took the best planning and coordination, multiple testing to family members and ourselves, and extreme cleaning measures, and we were able to visit the DR. When there is a will, you make things happen.

As the first semester of 2021 ended, our daughter Isabella finished her junior year with high honors, and it was about time to start looking for colleges. We thought she would pick marketing as a career, and I even introduced her to some contacts to apply for internships in the field. She started playing soccer and taking piano lessons at the tender age of six, balancing both activities until she chose to dedicate her limited free time solely to advancing her piano and voice skills. Little did we know she wanted to redirect.

The months flew by, and during the summer of 2021 she approached us both, wanting to have a conversation. Isabella has expressive big brown eyes, and they were all teary as she crossed her arms and shook a bit.

"Mom, Dad, I don't know where to start."

We looked at her and panicked a little bit. "What's going on, Isa?"

She said, "I don't want to study marketing like you, Mom. It is not what I want."

I looked at her and smiled. "Isabella, you don't have to follow what I do. I want you to decide and be happy." My mind wandered back to what happened with my sister when my dad wanted her to study something she had no passion about.

"Mom, Dad… I want to study music. I want to go to a music school and be a songwriter and a performer. There, I said it!" She burst into tears. We all had teary eyes and hugged, and we reassured her how happy we were for her and how she had our full support.

Our daughter had discovered her passion! We thought it was a hobby, but more importantly, she was willing to have the courage to fight for it too.

Her entire application and portfolio had to change in less than five months to get to her dream school. Time was of the essence. She made all her efforts, portfolio, auditions, and credentials, and took even more extra-curricular activities. I had no idea how hard it is to create a portfolio and apply in this field and how complex this world is to navigate. You can call me a fish out of water. She did most things alone.

She was giving it her all, applied to the few colleges she wanted, and had the specifics of her desired major.

In December of 2021, on a cold Saturday morning, while visiting NYC with her friends, she got an email and called us. "Mom, Dad, I got accepted into Berklee College of Music! I can't believe it!"

She did it! We were so proud. This was another milestone moment as a family, and our efforts were turning into wins.

This leap is giant and is the power of passion, perseverance, and determination.

You can always pivot and redirect, give it your maximum focus, and achieve even greater things you wouldn't imagine.

THE TWO-WAY DOORS

I asked my dear friend, Laura Schwartz, to share her personal story and career journey. Laura is the founder and CEO of 12 Leadership, an executive coaching and leadership development company, and the host of the podcast *MOJO Mondays*. She pivoted from a very successful career at American Express in marketing to start her own business. Laura grew up with amazing parents who were successful in their careers but not enjoying them. This gave her the drive to start her business and pursue her passion, and she has been doing so for the last fourteen years.

I interviewed Laura over the summer. Her strawberry blonde hair and great smile transmits that warmth in her. We started the conversation discussing if she intentionally planned this change in her life. "There was a lot of planning, but there also was tremendous serendipity, particularly in how I wound up at American Express, which is where I worked for almost a decade and built an incredibly strong and loyal network that ultimately became my clients at i2 Leadership."

Laura briefly paused, then continued, "However, joining American Express was never on my radar. I shared my plans of leaving my advertising job to pursue my MBA with a friend over dinner. She told me, 'Wait, you would be perfect for my job. I'm taking a new job, and they're looking for someone with your background.' I applied for the job, and three weeks later, I was at American Express. There was no intentionality there, and that changed the trajectory of my life."

One concept I found interesting from our conversation that can give us a new perspective and help us have the courage to change or pivot is what Laura calls "two-way door" decisions, the chance to reverse or pivot a decision without tremendous consequences. We treat lots of decisions as one-way doors. Once we go through them, we cannot undo the decision without significant consequences. And we lose a lot of time and opportunities because we become risk-averse and think we can't go back or pivot after we go through that door. We are afraid to leave a job if it doesn't work out. So rather than saying yes, we say no. We pass because we are unsure unless we feel 100 percent confident, which rarely happens, so we stay put and miss out on opportunities.

Laura encourages people to really assess, "Am I deciding to make a one-way door or a two-way door decision," because, most of the time, it is a two-way door.

We continued our conversation around being able to take action to overcome challenges and take advantage of opportunities. Laura reminds us of the importance of keeping our momentum going. She said, "Newton's law of physics motion talks about how an object at rest stays at rest. And you need to take action if you want a different outcome. If you want to change your circumstances or have a different outcome, you need a different approach."

You need to change your playbook, and you must be intentional about it. It just doesn't happen on its own.

"And that is one of the more significant differences between starting your own business and working for an organization. The self-discipline is at a whole other level. Yes, there's accountability. There you're trying to hit certain targets. But you really have a lot more control over your day and how you spend your time, and time gets consumed very, very quickly, as we know. And if you don't have the routines and structures to keep you focused, it can be a real impediment that will hinder your growth and ability to scale," she said.

Find your passion. Identify your superpowers
and what is it you're good at.

Have the determination and grit to leap into the life you want. This is easier said than done. That is why there are three important strategies to include in your tool kit, and we will dive into the first one, which is being a constant learner, in the following chapter.

Leaper's Tip

Think about what is in your way to the life you want and reflect on these questions:

- Are you comfortable with ambiguity and making decisions without the complete information set?

- Can you think about decisions you've made in the past and if you were overthinking them too much that caused inertia?

- Do you fall prey of analysis paralysis?

- Do you feel happy and fulfilled with the life you have and the work you are doing now? Do you feel stuck in the same place and don't have the courage to provoke the change?

- Have you turned down an opportunity and preferred to play it safe and stay where you are?

- Define your obstacles and challenges that are getting in the way to your success.

- Reflect about moments you have found that inner strength to pivot and write down the strategies and routines that worked for you and you used to persevere.

- Build a list of what you consider are your superpowers to keep persevering to achieve your goals. If you are unclear of which they are, ask your circle of trusted friends and relatives to identify them and share with you.

CHAPTER 8

STRATEGY #3: BEING A CONSTANT LEARNER: SHIFTING YOUR MINDSET

––––––––

"The people who are crazy enough to think they can change the world are the ones who do."

—STEVE JOBS

SCIENCE OF A GROWTH MINDSET: BECOMING A CONSTANT LEARNER

A growth mindset believes one can develop abilities and intelligence through dedication, effort, and a willingness to embrace challenges. It involves viewing failures and setbacks as opportunities for learning and personal growth.

I spent six months flying back and forth before bringing my family to the US. We are a tight family and always like doing things together. Still searching for a job, my husband didn't have a reference to work in the US even though he used to work for US companies while living abroad. My husband is a computer science engineer and has managed large organizations at national banks with complex IT infrastructure. Still, the challenge in front of him posed a different issue: Who would be willing to give him a chance?

He had a great idea of enrolling in a project management program at a college nearby to accelerate his job search and networking purposes. This also helped him get a certification in project management, which is an appreciated skill and is transferable to any industry or area if he had issues finding a job in tech. This helped him get a US college credential, and it also connected him to a new group of professionals, ideas, and a sense of accomplishment that brought him new fuel.

When the opportunity came in through a dear friend's recommendation, he took it and landed in a big consulting company. He got himself exposed to working with impressive accounts, and after several years a big energy infrastructure company offered him a senior role in one of the areas he enjoys the most within the CIO organization. His openness to try a new area to learn something new led him to greater success later, with new transferable skills along the way.

There are two types of mindsets: the fixed and the growth mindset. As a leaper, you will be in a growth mindset.

If you find yourself in a fixed mindset, don't worry. It is a process, and you will get there. This is already in you. You only need the appropriate tools, more information about these tools, and an openness to the concept.

That is the only requirement.

Leapers recognize they are an unfinished product. Life is a continuous journey of growth and development, and as professionals and leaders, we are no exception. In a constantly evolving world, staying relevant and effective as a leader requires a commitment to being a constant learner.

As Dr. Carol S. Dweck, a renowned psychologist and thought leader on the topic, explains in her Stanford Alumni address in 2014, "In a growth mindset, challenges are exciting rather than threatening. So, rather than thinking, 'Oh, I'm going to reveal my weaknesses,' you say, 'Wow, here's a chance to grow.'" This encapsulates the essence of a growth mindset, emphasizing the enthusiasm for challenges and recognizing their potential for personal development.

In her speech, Dr. Dweck talks about what she calls the "Power of Yet."

> I learned in high school in Chicago, where students had to pass eighty-four units to graduate. And if they didn't pass, they got the grade, not yet. I thought, isn't that wonderful? Because if you fail, you're nowhere. But if you get the grade not yet, you're on a learning curve. Not yet gave them a path into the future (Dweck 2014).

This reminded me that multiple times in my life, when someone would ask me if I was part of a specific social club, had my master's, had made manager, or learned to play a sport, I would always respond to them if I haven't achieved those goals with "Not yet."

It is powerful indeed.

It's the recognition that you do not know everything and still have much to learn and grow. You are chasing a better version of yourself as an unfinished product that refines with time.

This reminded me of a story from my mom. While still working for a big telecom company many years ago, she participated in a workshop and shared a story I have kept repeating to my kids, students, and teams throughout the years. In this workshop, the facilitator gets a white paper out of his desk drawer and shows them the white page with a dot painted in the center. He started asking the ones in the room, "What do you see here?" and all participants responded one by one, "I see a dot." Then, he said: "I showed you an entire page, and you can only see the dot."

It is up to you to recognize the immensity of the white page versus the dot on the page.

CHALLENGES MAKE YOU LEARN AND GROW STRONGER

While interviewing for the VP Job in New York, I recall one of the toughest interviews from many was from this head of sales for the carrier and wholesale team. I was waiting in a conference room of one of the buildings at the Bethpage location on Long Island, located on the first floor next to the human resources team. I was left by myself in complete silence, and I could hear my own heartbeat and a pin drop. Suddenly, the door opened, and a man wearing jeans and a jacket entered the room with a smile. I thought, *He doesn't seem as intimidating.* This started well.

He introduced himself and how he came from a financial background, and he dived into the numbers conversation and asked typical questions about my career, challenges, and experience. He then looked me in the eye, his face turned serious with a frowning forehead, and asked me this question: "You are coming from a small country and company. Aren't you afraid of managing ten times the budget you are responsible for now? And you think you can handle it and get us there?" It was still a valid question. Nevertheless, I had the drive to be there.

"I am not afraid. I'm encouraged by the challenge, and I know I can do it. I will apply myself using what I know from the business all these years and from my experience, and if I don't know an answer, I will say I don't know. But you can rest assured I will be relentless to seek and ask until I get the answer." To this day, I cherish our working relationship and accomplishments while being part of the same team.

Leapers are not afraid of challenges. We use them as fuel, and if there is something we cannot manage, we will find the way. These are often moments of reflection where we find ourselves wondering how to incorporate this in our daily lives.

Here is a list of phrases that I use and can support you in making that switch.

Fixed Mindset	Growth Mindset
"I don't know how to do this."	"I don't know yet, but I will learn and get better."
"I can't do it."	"I will try a different approach."
"I will fail at this."	"This is a learning opportunity for me."
"This is hard to do."	"I will practice and get better at it."
"They left me for last."	"I have more time to prepare."
"I don't like to be challenged."	"Challenges help me grow."
"I don't know how to do this."	"I don't know yet, I will learn and get better"
"I can't make this any better."	"I can always improve. I'll keep trying new strategies."
"It's too hard."	"This is challenging, but I can tackle it step by step."
"I made a mistake."	"Mistakes help me learn and grow."
"I'll never be as smart as them."	"I can learn from others and develop my own strengths."
"This is good enough. I don't need to try harder."	"Is there a way to improve this further? I can always grow."
"I give up."	"I haven't figured it out yet, but I will keep trying."
"It's not my fault I failed."	"What can I learn from this experience to do better next time?"
"This success was just luck."	"My effort led to this success. I will continue to grow."
"I don't like to be challenged."	"Challenges help me grow and improve."

HOW BEING OPEN TO CHANGES CAN TRANSFORM YOUR LIFE AND BRING MEANINGFUL IMPACT TO OTHERS

I thought about bringing an example of game-changers with a growth mindset to interview, and the name Claudia Romo Edelman, the founder of We Are All Human—a non-profit to advance diversity and inclusion—came about. Claudia has over twenty-five years of experience in humanitarian causes and driving social change; and has worked with organizations such as the United Nations, UNICEF, UNHCR, and the World Economic Forum.

Her journey began amidst the chaos and destruction of the earthquakes in Mexico City, where she first discovered her innate ability to lead and make an impact. As a teenager, she found herself amidst a group of adults, sweeping the streets, searching for survivors. "I remember to start yelling very loud, stop, stop, stop let's go back, I hear a voice," Claudia recalls. This moment where she rallied others to rescue a trapped girl and twenty others encapsulated Claudia's realization that her voice and actions could bring significant change.

"When I was a little girl people understood that I was not going to survive long, and I was always under a microscope since my two other siblings had developed this disease from a rare genetic incompatibility and died at the age of eighteen months. Despite the odds and the optics, I survived!" she said. This experience gave her the strength to see the world through the lens of opportunity and that she can achieve anything she proposes to do.

Claudia's story is not just about overcoming adversity. It's about transforming challenges into opportunities for growth and impact.

She moved from Mexico to Switzerland with her family in a diplomatic mission. In Switzerland, the educational system's rigidity almost confined her daughter to a predetermined path, and that is when she relocated to work in the US. Now, her daughter has flourished and even accomplished giving a speech at the US Congress.

She then asked, "Mirna, did you see *Barbie*, the movie?"

"I did and loved it!" I responded.

She continued, "I believe we need to start from a position of awareness. I think the America Ferrara moment, when she breaks the spell, is the awakening moment for women to see our value and power to move forward. It is the same feeling I have for how, as Latinos, we need to see ourselves and change the perceptions from takers to makers. I am a data-driven marketer, and Latinos are a big force of movement for the economy, and that is what the data in America says."

Her legacy is not just in the tangible changes she has brought to life. She sets an example for aspiring change-makers, especially in the Latino community. "As a Latina and an entrepreneur, I bring a unique blend of passion, perseverance, and optimism to my work. I ensure I understand all aspects before proceeding with a change. Discipline, routines, and structured planning are essential for turning big ideas into realistic plans."

Her story is a powerful reminder of how overcoming obstacles and driving meaningful change is possible with resilience, strategic thinking, and a deep understanding of one's roots and identity.

A BETTER VERSION OF YOURSELF

Being intentional is as important as it is to develop the right mindset. If you have a growth mindset, you see rejections, failures, and obstacles as lessons, something you can learn from and then build a new roadmap for future wins.

Consider Ney Díaz, who is the CEO and president of INTRAS, a highly recognized training and development company in the Caribbean, Spain, and Latin America. I had a conversation with Ney, one of the best professors I had back in college in the Dominican Republic, and he has successfully created a new category for the region throughout the years with tremendous success. The first thing I noticed behind him in our Zoom call was his extensive library of books and the amazing charisma that is so characteristic of him.

We discussed how he created and scaled his business from scratch as an idea he took from his mother while working as a general manager for a big firm. "The idea of starting this business came from the need to generate additional revenues, as I was getting married." We both laughed. "This is how it all started. I asked this firm if they were okay with it, and they said yes. Imagine if I hadn't asked and stayed just business as usual."

He later decided he had a niche in his hands, providing a unique value proposition of specialized content for the market, and quit his well-compensated job to pursue this dream full-time. Fast forward to today, he has created a reference for himself and his company, launching other divisions, including a leadership magazine and a podcast series. He is also a published author of *The Twelve Questions*. We discussed a story in his book about an experience with Seth Godin, a speaker for one of his events in the Dominican Republic. He noticed Seth carrying an apple before starting the conference. Ney thought, *I hope he eats it before approaching the podium.* He did not (Diaz 2022).

Seth addressed the audience with the following message: He looked up that a banana is a primary product the Dominican Republic exports. In this hotel buffet, they were offering apples, which are imported goods. He said how a perfect occasion to showcase the DR's great organic banana product this event presented to the hotel and yet decided to go with the less risky option that everybody would like. "That's how 99 percent of the people behave, going with the traditional that everyone likes and not the unconventional. That's why you have millions of businesses and only one Google, one Amazon, and one Apple."

Ney is also a believer of supporting others in their growth path. "I will stop doing anything if somebody calls me for advice and has the courage to ask for help and wants to learn." If I would have realized this earlier in my career and entrepreneurship journey, I would have gotten even farther and much faster. We must be constant learners to grow.

If you have a fixed mindset, you will always complain about rejections. You always complain about things that go bad but never find a way to improve upon them. When you have a growth mindset, you see the possibilities and opportunities if something does not go as expected or you see mistakes as learning opportunities.

Having a growth mindset is what kept me and my family going. At this point in our lives, we had completely adapted our new environment and culture. We had also survived a pandemic in the process—that brought learnings to all of us—helping us value family and our life from a different perspective and becoming stronger.

Our kids are way ahead in achieving the milestones we set for ourselves before moving to New York. Ivan is now living in New York City, finishing up his studies at NYU, and Isabella is living in Boston, where she gave us a gastronomic tour, from their iconic Mexican tacos place to their Italian restaurants in Newbury Street, both independent. My husband and I are also fulfilling our own milestones as professionals and parents and preparing for our next stage as empty nesters. And we keep on learning.

As Matthew McConaughey well said in his Best Actor Oscar acceptance speech at the Academy Awards in 2014: "You see, every day, and every week, and every month, and every year of my life, my hero is always ten years away. I'm never going to be my hero. I'm not going to obtain that... and that's fine with me because it keeps me with somebody to keep on chasing" (McConaughey 2014).

Having a growth mindset is to keep chasing that hero, that better version of ourselves, that will be thankful ten years from now that we opened our hearts and minds to learn constantly.

Moreover, pursuing knowledge equips us with a broader perspective, allowing us to navigate adversity with resilience, adaptability, and an abundance mindset.

As you reflect on your life journey and are more aware of where you are and where you want to go next, based on your definition of success, this will be an essential tool when you are going through changes in your life. In the following chapter, I will bring two topics that you can leverage for leaping out of your lane as it prepares you for confronting the risks that come with it: resilience and self-confidence.

Leaper's Tip

As we recognize that we do not know it all and are an unfinished product, here are some recommendations on cultivating a growth mindset shared with my #LeapersMindset community that can help you on your personal life as well as your leadership journey:

Curate your learning path.	Identify the areas where you want to grow and excel. Seek books, courses, webinars, and mentors who can help you expand your knowledge and skill set. Don't wait for opportunities to come to you—actively pursue them!
Embrace failure as a learning opportunity.	Remember, setbacks are steppingstones to success. When you stumble, don't let it discourage you. Instead, analyze what went wrong, extract valuable lessons, and apply them to future endeavors.
Encourage a culture of learning.	As a leader, you must foster a learning-friendly environment within your team or organization. Promote knowledge sharing, provide resources for skill development, and encourage open dialogue. When your team grows, so does your capacity to achieve greatness.

CHAPTER 9

STRATEGY #4: BUILDING RESILIENCE AND SELF-CONFIDENCE

"Don't ever let someone tell you, you can't do something. Not even me. You got a dream, you got to protect it. People can't do something themselves; they want to tell you can't do it. You want something, go get it."

—WILL SMITH, AS CHRIS GARDNER, IN THE PURSUIT OF HAPPYNESS.

We had to adapt, build resilience, and have courage every day to conquer our goals in America.

We had to adapt. I had to adapt. That is to live in a city where the train and the MTA are of the essence to your everyday life, and you learn to have respect for the word "commuting." If it snows, the tropical sun of the Caribbean is a distant memory. It's a whole new level of planning.

I finally understood why rental cars always come with a brush and scraper, and then getting off at the Hicksville train station back from work past 7:00 p.m. and run to a dark—sometimes sketchy—Long

Island Rail Road parking lot. Also, you cannot find your car, since it's sitting like a shapeless mound under a thick blanket of white snow. The car alarm becomes handy, and the defrost button, too, when your hands are numb while scraping your windshield. As I fumbled with the scraper and breaths visible in the frosty air, I'd catch myself again wondering, *What am I doing here?*

I'm here to become a stronger person, a stronger mom, and a professional. I'm here to get out of my comfort zone and to carry the dreams of many of us in our developing countries, the ones already in America, and the millions of Americans who started small or their parents and have big aspirations. To remind me and remind them that is possible.

After our first few years, we were still figuring things out as a family, and that is okay. You don't need to have it all figured out to leap out, but you certainly need a plan and the determination to execute it. We were following the plan, absorbing changes and challenges as we kept building our resilience, an important asset to triumph to changes.

BUILDING RESILIENCE: NAVIGATE ADVERSITY WITH STRENGTH AND ADAPTABILITY

According to the American Psychological Association (APA), resilience can be defined as the process and outcome of successfully adapting to complex or challenging life experiences, especially through mental, emotional, and behavioral flexibility and adjustment to external and internal demands. They also suggest the level of how well we can cope with these challenges depends on certain factors around how we engage with the world, the social resources around us, and how we lean into coping strategies to help us move on (American Psychological Association 2018).

It reminds me of a Kelly Clarkson song I reference to my team members, colleagues, and even bosses I've had in the past: "What doesn't kill you makes you stronger." One of my team members once told me, "You will become a real New Yorker when you: scrape your car windshield, start swearing when you get a blizzard and must plow, and the other one is… falling on the pavement on black ice."

Boom! Done that.

It was wintertime, and I recently moved to our new headquarters office building in Long Island City Tower. I started commuting almost daily, heading at 7:00 a.m. to the new offices, and one day it was snowing. From my office window on the forty-seventh floor, I could see the snow covering the streets and the building roofs. I could also see the breathtaking billion-dollar Manhattan skyline with icons such as the Empire State Building and the Brooklyn Bridge. Makes you feel you are on top of the world, even if you don't want to be. It is such an unprecedented feeling for me.

It seemed one of those days when train delays were inevitable, and my goal was to reach home as early as possible. I aimed for the 6:08 p.m. train, knowing I needed at least thirteen minutes to race to Hunterspoint Avenue train station. Exiting the building later than planned, urgency kicked in. If I were to catch the train on time, I needed to run, or as my kids would say, "dash"—though hindsight would reveal that perhaps this was not the wisest decision.

With urgency as my rhythm, I started running and repeating in my head, *I must make it on time! Go, go, go!* I made a turn to Jackson Avenue. The pavement was treacherous, and I started feeling like I was going through a soapy and wet floor. *Don't slow down, Mirna. Keep focus.* I suddenly tripped, lost balance, and slipped!

I fell on the pavement. It was inevitable. I thought, *Oh no, what an embarrassment!* Then I felt something. "Ouch!" My knee had a bruise and a red scarlet stream of blood running down my black pantyhose. As I laid there, contemplating the ignominy of my spill, two strangers—a middle-aged man and a young woman—emerged from the anonymity of the city, extending hands not just of assistance but of shared humanity in the concrete wilderness.

They asked, "Are you okay?" as they helped me incorporate and get up.

"I'm okay. Thank you, I'll manage."

I got up. *I will manage it.* My feelings were taking over. *I must keep it together.* I felt the tears in my eyes. *What am I doing here in this wintery place? I'm a Caribbean girl!*

I started crying as I walked slowly to the train and started to limp, a slight but persistent reminder of the fall, until I got to the train station. I missed the train and had to wait for the next one, and it felt like the longest ride getting back to Long Island.

During the train ride, I had time to think and reassess. What happened here as a product of the growing pains of living in a new environment. It doesn't feel good, but wait… now I made it to a true New Yorker status. It's a milestone instead of a fall! I then started to laugh.

My husband, Ivan, waited for me at the Hicksville train station. "What happened to you? Oh, God!"

I responded with a big chuckle. "I fell on the pavement in front of everyone. It's official—I'm a true New Yorker now!"

To build resilience, you can laugh and talk about yourself and your mistakes with some humor. It is picking yourself up, letting go, and moving on as a stronger person. You must also be intentional about it, an essential quality to every leader, and I would even say every person. The pandemic years of COVID-19 and its impact on mental health issues have made it a challenge for any human in this society. More so, resilience is key in any leadership journey as in everyday life, like feeling confident as an athlete who gets drafted or exchanged to a new team. You will throw yourself into new situations and feel, as I always say, "Comfortable with being uncomfortable."

When we cultivate resilience and make this part of our lifestyle, we will bounce back from setbacks stronger than ever and thrive in situations of adversity.

When we moved to New York, little did we know my brother-in-law back in DR would be going through cancer and that we would be going through that terrible year of not being physically there to support him. If it weren't for the help of others around us, our faith, the resilience we had built so far, and our family bond, it would have taken a much bigger toll on us.

You may be going through your own struggles right now, such as being at a crossroads wanting to change careers, losing your job, not getting that promotion or seed capital, not getting accepted to the school you wanted, ending a difficult relationship, or something as traumatic such as losing a loved one. As we continue to explore the complexities of resilience, ongoing research contributes to our understanding of the factors that promote hardiness, providing valuable insights into how we can develop and harness this essential trait in our lives.

The three resilience types you can reflect on and explore are ones I learned through my research, personal experience, and conversations with other successful leaders.

Emotional Resilience

Developing emotional intelligence, practicing self-compassion, and cultivating a growth mindset are essential for building emotional resilience. Experts also recommend recognizing and managing one's emotions, seeking support from a supportive network, and engaging in activities that promote self-care and stress reduction. This plays a crucial role in maintaining psychological well-being.

To become a leaper, you must also build a special capacity to "move on." This has been an essential trait for me that builds over time. You close a chapter and open a new one, and you build that resilience to the extent it gives you so much adrenaline every time you go through a change.

Cognitive Resilience

It involves building mental fortitude and adaptability in the face of challenges. Wiseseed emphasizes the importance of cognitive flexibility, stating, "Resilient individuals reframe adversity and see it as an opportunity for growth." Adopting a positive style without it being toxic, challenging negative thoughts, and developing problem-solving skills are vital for developing cognitive resilience. Engaging in activities that foster creativity, such as writing or painting, can also enhance cognitive flexibility and resilience (Wiseseed 2020).

My friend Sharon McDowell-Larsen, PhD, wrote the article, "Fueling the Brain: From Exhausted to Energized." In it, she talks about mental fatigue, the psychobiological state of tiredness that makes your brain foggy and slows you down, and it is a state caused by prolonged periods of demanding cognitive activity (Mcdowell-Larsen 2021).

This can come on gradually and is cumulative. However, various factors such as sleep, diet, exercise, meditation, and nature can help with brain fatigue and recovery. Something that works for me and takes me to a wonderland of feelings is music and dancing. It's a therapy by itself and has a healing power every time. Do you have a playlist that uplifts you or makes you disconnect? If not yet, try it and start crafting your playlists to use music as a healer.

Physical Resilience

This one is closely intertwined with mental and emotional well-being and contributes significantly to overall resilience. As researcher George A. Kuchel notes, "Physical resilience, which we define as one's ability to withstand or recover from functional decline after an acute or chronic health stressor, is a construct that resonates with older adults and caregivers. Successful aging often depends on a person's response to the inevitability of late-life stressors" (Kuchel et al. 2018, 1459–1461).

Exercise, adequate sleep, and healthy eating habits are essential for maintaining physical resilience. This will help us keep our vitality as we go through life changes.

BUILD AND INCORPORATE RESILIENCE INTO YOUR LIFE

Nurturing meaningful connections, fostering supportive relationships, and seeking help from others when needed are crucial for building resilience. Building a strong support network through family, friends, or communities provides a foundation of care and encouragement during difficult times.

I asked Lucy Chen, the author of *Build Resilience: Live, Learn, and Lead*, what her definition of resilience is, and I loved it. She said, "Resilience is forging ahead despite obstacles, finding brilliance in challenges, persisting with dreams in your heart, one step at a time."

As a working mom, executive, and high-performance professional with stress being a big part of what I had to handle throughout my career journey, one key action I learned from successful leaders is how to invest in myself by booking relaxing massages, coachings, and activities to de-compress on a weekly or monthly basis. I usually book massages or take a bubble bath to indulge myself and prevent burnout. I also take a break of a day or two to do something for me or with my family every six weeks.

Resilience is needed for every leader who lives in an environment of change and takes the leap into new challenges.

As I navigate this chapter in my life, right after COVID-19, I received a promotion to manage the company's $10 billion product portfolio, which is a milestone moment. As mounting pressure and the environment heated, I relegated eating healthy, understanding nutrition and portioning. As a result, I gained disproportionate weight and didn't feel good about myself. I contacted a dear friend, a coach in nutrition and wellness, and started a program.

My dear friend Wendy Madera is a psychologist, graduated cum laude from the Institute for Communication and Psychology in the Netherlands, and I started coaching sessions on nutrition with her. One day, I asked her to share her motivation to change from being a computer science graduate and successful tech professional to this new coaching career. Her motivation came through several health experiences with her family that almost took a toll on her if it wasn't for her emotional resilience.

I asked Wendy to share her personal story that took her to this transition in her life and established her coaching practice for high-performance women executives.

"Two years after my husband overcame colon cancer, we found ourselves back in the hospital, this time grappling with every parent's worst nightmare: A ten-centimeter tumor had been discovered in the abdominal cavity of our five-year-old daughter—and our worlds collapsed. A tsunami of stress, anxiety, sorrow, and anguish overwhelmed me."

In this moment of crisis, Wendy gained a new perspective on what mattered in life. Her body's fight-or-flight response activated as a primal reaction beneficial for survival but was disproportionate in this situation. She concluded she had to accept it to support her daughter rather than fighting or fleeing from reality.

"This was because 80 percent of our body's defense system is in the digestive tract, and stress thins the intestinal walls. This makes it easier for toxic bacteria and viruses to permeate and alter our gut flora. Moreover, the food available at the hospital was far from healthy. It's crucial to understand that our microbe's sense when the brain is stressed, worried, angry, anxious—they don't just listen. They directly influence our emotions."

Through our conversation, I discovered stress and poor nutrition are the perfect mix to alter the state of your gut flora and, consequently, your emotional state. Drawing an analogy with *Star Wars*, she describes the gut flora as a battleground between good and evil forces.

"You know the movie *Star Wars*? Imagine that within our gut flora reside the 'forces of good' and the 'forces of evil.' The forces of evil exist even in healthy gut flora because they have a specific job to do. The issue arises when, due to stress and poor diet, the 'forces of evil' grow while the 'forces of good' diminish. This leads to significant inflammation in the body. Knowing this, one must act accordingly. Hence, I made changes to enhance my resilience," Wendy said.

Realizing this, she took steps such as getting homemade food from her husband every day instead of hospital food, sleeping at home some days for better rest, reading for mental peace, walking, and meditating.

Eventually, they discharged her daughter from the hospital. She reflects that if she hadn't taken care of herself, anxiety could have overwhelmed her, potentially leading to burnout.

You deserve to thrive. Hence, resilience
must be part of your leap plan.

Steven Southwick and Dennis Charney have studied resilient people for over twenty years, which they devoted to studying the cases of Vietnam prisoners of war, Special Forces instructors, and civilians who dealt with experiences of abuse, trauma, and health. In their book, *Resilience: The Science of Mastering Life's Greatest Challenges*, they assembled the ten things resilient people must confront when life throws a curve ball or going through trauma. *Time* magazine listed them in their article about emotional resilience (Barker 2016). I added a summary below:

1. Be optimistic and look at the bright side.
2. Face your fears and throw yourself into uncomfortable situations.
3. Have a moral compass.
4. Practice spirituality or some community gathering.
5. Look for resilient role models.
6. Have physical resilience.
7. Keep your brain strong and be a lifelong learner.
8. Be cognitively flexible and use humor.
9. Find meaning in what you do.

As a couple and even as a family, we have been part of a community that works with families and marriages for almost twenty years. This work has allowed us and our kids to see hundreds of family situations and moments of distress. In every case, those who survived or improved their lives significantly had a will to advance, and they cultivated the resilience to make them stronger. Things didn't get better for them only. They also became much stronger and more confident as a family that they were a unit to last, nurture, and cherish.

I will always tell my kids this: "We are a family, and you are wearing a T-shirt with our last names imprinted in the back." Which means we are part of the same team. We don't leave a team member behind. We live by the same values, we take care of each other, and we strive to win.

CONFIDENCE: DRIVE YOUR STORY AND ADVOCATE FOR YOURSELF

To manage and incorporate change in our lives successfully, there is another important trait we need in our tool kit, and that is self-confidence.

I found this definition in an article by Tanya J. Peterson from Healthy Place valuable and accurate: "Self-confidence is the courage someone has to know himself, believe in himself, and act on those beliefs. Self-confidence is self-respect and positive self-regard. To improve self-confidence is to improve the quality of one's life" (Peterson, 2006).

An illustration of this is believing in what you do, being worthy of respect, accepting your strengths and weaknesses, and standing up for yourself. It is also interesting to see what self-confidence is not. It is not that you do everything perfectly and can't make mistakes or that you set unrealistic and demanding expectations of yourself.

When we identify our strengths and weaknesses,
we can build our self-confidence by accepting
our weaknesses, creating an improvement plan,
and celebrating our strengths by showcasing
our superpowers in our everyday lives.

Randi Braun is an executive coach and author of *The Wall Street Journal*'s best-selling book, *Something Major: The New Playbook for Women at Work*. In her book, she affirms, "Understanding our strengths doesn't just enhance our performance but gives us the confidence and clarity to handle our weaknesses—without letting them be existential." She makes a calling to start obsessing with our strengths and own our superpowers to develop a reservoir of positive knowledge about ourselves if we go through a confidence drought (Braun 2023, 44).

I gained a new perspective on confidence while meeting Lisa Sun at an event organized by Chief in NYC in the fall of 2023. She explained how her world turned from being an executive in a consulting firm for years in corporate America to a mission to provide every woman with the confidence she needed. Lisa started her fashion company, which would provide a dress tailored to women based on the special occasion celebrated to boost their confidence.

Around this being a support for overcoming the most difficult challenges we can face daily, she responded, "It doesn't get easier. It gets harder. You get stronger." I agreed wholeheartedly. Here, the pivoting moment started for her with a review from her former boss, saying she didn't have enough "gravitas" for a promotion and to make a partner. She discovered that confidence was behind this word and wrote a great book called *Gravitas* to help others through her story of building confidence.

And how can we gain confidence and advocate for ourselves? Sheena Yap is the author of *The Tao of Self Confidence*, a guide for Asian women to tap into their self-confidence. She goes through her personal story and how she overcame self-doubt to regain her confidence. I read the book to understand her story and found applicable advice and ideas to support building confidence. Her book provides a three-step approach to building self-confidence, starting with the first of just believing in yourself. This is the most important one, as you cannot move forward without this being clear to you. The second one is to educate yourself. The third is having a purpose (Yap 2023, 138–139).

Now that we understand that we must be constant learners and strive to become the best version of ourselves, taking care of ourselves, and building resilience and confidence to get ready to leap out, it is time for us to think about what will motivate us to make these changes: the purpose in our life.

Leaper's Tip

- Evaluate where you are in your levels of resilience: Emotional, cognitive, and physical. Seek guidance from a coach to help you if needed.
- Learn more about yourself through a confidence test available online or through your selected coach.
- Find more information to learn more about tools available to you through books, conferences, and support groups.

  Define a plan to start working in some of these areas and pace yourself. You will have better results if you focus.

PART 3

LEAPER'S BLUEPRINT

CHAPTER 10

STRATEGY #5: A PURPOSE-DRIVEN LIFE

"The two most important days of your life are… The day you were born and the day you find out why."

—MARK TWAIN.

Becoming a constant learner and knowing yourself deeply can lead to profound personal fulfillment. It can also lead to discovering the life purpose that will drive and keep us focused on our goals, whatever they are.

As a trait that is core to a leaper, being able to leap out of your lane means you need a connection of dots through your life-changing moments. A leaper uses this opportunity to "leap out" as a defining moment that is a catalyst for growth, using purpose as a compass.

When talking about meaning and purpose through introspection, we gain clarity about our passions and purpose, aligning our actions with our values and goals. This alignment enhances our fulfillment and satisfaction, creating a meaningful, purpose-driven life.

Leapers have a very clear sense of purpose in life, and despite the different experiences they throw themselves into, they choose to accept and gravitate toward this sense of meaning and purpose.

In our second year living in New York, we found ourselves with our son on his way to college, and we were still living on Long Island. I was working several days a week from the Bethpage office and the other part of the week from the Long Island City headquarters. My team and the business division were having the best year of growth, and the strategy we implemented was working to help fuel our positive results. The comeback and rebuilding of the product portfolio weren't quite easy, but we made it happen as a team.

The year started strong, and the phones were ringing again in our call center with the recently released campaign and over-performing budget. Kevin called me into his office with excellent news.

"Mirna, you've just being promoted to senior vice president, and we will add an expanded scope of responsibilities and actions, including setting up a new e-commerce channel for businesses."

Here we go! Transformation 2.0 started with great news and new challenges to conquer.

On the personal side, after my brother-in-law passed away from cancer, it was a challenging period to go through work and school and continue to adapt to this new culture and environment. We missed our family and friends to support us to cope with the loss, and above all I needed to support my husband who didn't want to go out to dinner or even watch a play or movie.

To get us back on our feet, my team at work came up with a caring and thoughtful idea. They bought several gift cards from different restaurants, enough for going out for an entire month. They created a suggested route for us to follow and provided recommendations of what to order, menus, specials, and more. They wanted us to experience joy and go out again, experiencing life itself.

I will always be grateful to my team. The strategy started to work, and we were out and about going at our own pace. Being so far away from family and friends, it was hard to remember our brother was gone and we wouldn't see him again every time.

At that moment, I realized the power of one of the goals and the vision I have clearly defined as part of my sense of purpose: to support others and provide guidance in times of turmoil or when the opportunity presents itself. I also realized what I've been saying throughout the years became a reality. It is tremendously important to create a supportive environment, to have an impact on others. One phrase I always entertain and share with my teams:

We must be that beacon of light and hope, amid confusion, uncertainty, or any circumstances.

At this moment in time, I thought about the accomplishments so far. I started gaining some perspective from self-reflection about how our journey of moving to the US contributed, or not, to what I defined as my purpose in life. There are specific steps to get there and find your true calling and, most importantly, what your definition of success is. Going from our second to the third year, it was clear some of the milestones we defined as success factors (key performance indicators are not only for your work-related projects) were accomplished. Your family and personal life is your most precious assets, most inspiring piece of work, and most meaningful business.

Studies have shown that having a clear sense of purpose contributes to overall well-being and resilience. In the United States, where the pursuit of happiness is deeply ingrained in the national psyche, finding meaning in life becomes even more significant. According to a Gallup poll conducted in 2021, only 33 percent of Americans are engaged in their jobs, indicating that many individuals may need a sense of purpose in their professional lives. This highlights the need for individuals to explore their passions and align with their "why" (Harter 2022).

In contemporary society, where mental health issues and existential concerns are on the rise, the pursuit of a life purpose becomes increasingly relevant. According to Johns Hopkins Medicine, an estimated 26 percent of Americans ages eighteen and older—about one in four adults—suffer from a diagnosable mental disorder in a given year. Having a sense of purpose can serve as a protective factor against mental health challenges, providing individuals with a sense of meaning and motivation to navigate the ups and downs of life. Finding one's life purpose is a critical aspect of personal growth and well-being, offering individuals a guide to navigating the complexities of life (Johns Hopkins 2023).

In fact, it extends to our work life, and taking from an article published by Gallup and written by Jake Herway in May 2021, organizations that succeed in making their mission personal to employees see performance that sets them apart. Gallup research shows 10 percent improvement in employees' connection with the mission or purpose of their organization leads to an 8.1 percent decrease in turnover and a 4.4 percent increase in profitability (Heraway 2023).

After careful analysis and several interviews with top executives and being in corporations for more than twenty years working with different cultures, I will say that defining your purpose is a building block in everything you do, and your personal and professional life as a leaper comes to these three steps.

Defining our why and core values is essential.

When interviewed in the Jordan Harbinger show in 2018, motivational speaker and multiple times best-selling author Simon Sinek made an interesting analogy using his life as an example.

> My *why* is to inspire people to do the things that inspire them so, together, each of us can change our world for the better. Now, I can do that in a million ways: I can write a book. I can give a talk. I can advise someone. That's who I am as a friend. That's who I am as a brother. That's who I am as a son. It's who I am. And my opportunity is to find the creative ways in which I can bring who I am and inject life into it.

When you understand and articulate your "why," you can create a sense of clarity, inspiration, and direction in your life. He encourages communicating your "why" effectively to inspire others, build trustworthy loyal relationships, and drive meaningful change to your life inspired by your why and your values (Harbinger 2018).

It reminds me of my conversation with my friend Stephanie Nuesi, who had learned English in just five years, turning herself into a powerhouse owner of her company Max Up at twenty-four. She wanted to build a legacy to honor her parents and help others. That gave her a sense of purpose aligned with her values and beliefs. Though, what she was pursuing was something she hasn't done before and a significantly different path from where she was six years earlier. She gave a voice to all the entry-level workers after building over 250,000 followers on LinkedIn.

"I want to leave a legacy. My parents sacrificed—my mother left everything back—to give me the opportunities I had. I need to now pay it forward to others and make it my life purpose," Stephanie concluded.

Throughout my career, I received many trainings on defining your core values, which helped me shape into the leaper I am today. I won't bail on or disregard these values, no matter the culture I'm in or the company or boss I'm working for. I carry and treasure these non-negotiable values, such as honesty, integrity, compassion, responsibility, authenticity, honor, and dignity.

To thrive through challenges and get out of your comfort zone, you must establish clear values to support your journey.

These values can be influenced by your faith or beliefs; your family and friends around you; or even your school, teachers, major events that happened in your life, and many others. Your values also reflect your beliefs, what motivates you, and what you want to focus on or champion.

I decided to sit down for a conversation with my dear friend Kevin Stephens. As you can recall he was the one who gave me the opportunity and was the conduit for offering to relocate me and my family to US. Kevin is the chairman of the board for various Fortune 100 companies and someone I can personally attest is a leaper and a successful executive, mentor, and dear friend. I've known Kevin for almost eight years and reported to him for almost three years while being EVP and president of business for a large telecom and cable company in New York.

Despite his busy schedule being a board member, every time I need clarity and mentorship, Kevin is there. This extends not only to me, but to my family as well. For Kevin, his faith and family are sacred, and he is one of the most coherent people I've ever met, true to his values and beliefs.

At the end of a long workday for me, I got to my home office and logged into the video call. He is in Texas Pacific time while I'm on Eastern standard time in New York.

"Hey, Kevin. Great to see you. What's going on? Thanks for doing this," I said.

"All good, great to see you, Mirna. Glad to help," Kevin said with a big smile. For me it felt as if I was calling my big brother for his advice. That is what sponsors, more than a mentor, make you feel. Sponsors are those champions in our lives who are there for us as a sounding board, a guiding light, or a cheerleader.

"I've known many things in your professional life, Kevin. Let's start with your life journey."

"All right. I was wondering how back you want me to go?" he said.

"Take it away, Kevin. I want to know the story," I said.

"One of my earliest memories, as the oldest of three kids, is while my father was in the army. He was away for the first two years of my life, and my mother and I were living with my grandparents and her siblings, so I was the only kid living in the house in this crazy environment with all these adults. I needed to be mature early on, in a weird kind of way," Kevin said.

As he went on in our conversation, what he said next surprised me.

"Fast forward a few years, I remember distinctly my father came back from deployment, and we were living in our own house where I was going to school. I was in second grade. And I remember coming home and asking my parents to move. I told them, 'I want to go to a different school. I don't like my school.'"

The reason is that he grew up in an urban environment in Detroit, Michigan. He remembers vividly walking home from school and seeing kids fighting and engaging in chaotic behavior. "I just saw chaos. And at that early age, I knew I didn't like chaos," Kevin said.

The event steered his childhood in a new direction. At a young age, he urged his parents to seek a pivot, leaving behind an environment at odds with his identity and values.

He recounted another defining moment: getting lost in an amusement park at night while with his cousins and aunt. This experience taught him that succumbing to stress or uncertainty would cloud his judgment. He learned his best strategy in such situations was to seek help from a police officer. Following this approach led to a swift reunion with his family.

"It was an early indicator of, you know, what do you do when things go wrong?" Kevin said. "I ended up understanding that God had something in store for me. In many cases that required me to make a change, either where I was living, working, what I was doing. And if you're willing to embrace that change, it doesn't mean you just wing it. You do some preparation. If you're willing to embrace that change, then God will fulfill his promise that he'll take care of you."

As a result of those two incidents, Kevin almost rinsed and repeated them in his early childhood, his career changes, and for the rest of his life. Those early life events were memorable to him and set a foundation for figuring out and pivoting to being purposeful and trusting God.

DISCOVERING AND DEFINING YOUR PURPOSE

My mom, Elvira, always said you must be the main character of your story; the lead character of the movie you call your life. She instilled in me the sense of driving toward something beyond ourselves and having *healthy ambitions*. I call "healthy ambitions" the targets or goals you set that will not only support your definition of success but will also positively impact the lives of others and the world around you. One characteristic of a healthy ambition is looking at the impact it leaves on you and others. If the effect is positive and is leaving the world around you better, then you know it is healthy.

Also, these ambitions need a connection with your core values and beliefs. Your core values guide you to define your ambitions and how they transform throughout time. This is key to being a leaper, since you are not just driving your life through different experiences. While you do that, you keep true to your core values and life purpose, which gives a whole different meaning to leaping out of your lane. It's not about project hopping or job hopping. It's about being intentional and ensuring you are clear in your values and life purpose as a compass. Each step is a building block of your journey. This lens will evaluate each change that comes your way.

As my conversation with Kevin continued, I discovered that when he lived in Michigan, he went to college to study business, concentrating in marketing and finance, but he first started as a music major. His love for jazz gave him a nomination by his peers for an award in high school. Kevin said, "I played tenor saxophone and jazzman in a band of eighty musicians. It's the smallest little memento I'll show you from my high school years." He gets up and finds this small wooden trophy with a golden shape on top, and you can see in his eyes how much this meant to him. "This is the John Philip Sousa award that band members vote on the best musician in the band."

He went on to describe how he shifted from music to finance, how he got his first job in finance after proactively calling the recruiter and explaining he was the best fit for the job, and how he moved to LA, California. Three months into the job, the initial excitement faded.

The exact moment of realization was unclear, but his proficiency in math led him there. Soon, he recognized that finance represented going from spreadsheet to spreadsheet and did not align with his true motivators, nor did it represent where he wanted to invest his life's efforts.

"And then something happened," he said. "I ran into these guys who were in sales and marketing. They were driving Porsches to work and wearing fancy clothes. And they seemed to be just the ultimate cool kind of people." He decided to pivot and give sales a try. He continued, "This time, I did better research, and a year later I moved into sales, and that was the beginning of my entire career."

He pivoted again. And as a good leaper, he studied every move through the lens of his core values and purpose. Kevin's core values were as clear as water, and he carried those core values to develop his successful career and craft his purpose along the way. It was steady, though not in a straight line, with intentionality and flexibility to mold and drive change when needed. That is how he became president in a Fortune 500 company and is now chairman of several boards in the US.

He is also a successful and loving parent of three amazing young adults with his charming wife, who is now enjoying this phase of their lives as empty nesters. Every time I see them and their kids, I see the joy and fulfillment of their life purpose.

PURPOSE AND MISSION

After our third year in the US, right before the COVID-19 pandemic hit the world by storm, I started supporting the Women's Affinity Groups at work as their executive sponsor. I've always advocated for women's leadership development and coaching. I did it through the girls program I developed with my sister and ran for ten years in DR. Part of my life purpose is tied to my core values and beliefs.

Purpose and vision are crafted over time, and certain events can mark a new chapter and help the leaper in you resurface and prompt change to pivot.

The Women's Affinity Group and the leadership for DEI came up with the idea of the first Women's Leadership Forum. As an executive sponsor and part of the leadership team, I would participate in the main panel of discussion for the summit. The forum had employees and students from under-represented or disadvantaged schools on Long Island. A prominent group of women in the area included: the Nassau County Executive, the newly appointed DA, our chief diversity officer, and myself representing the women executives of the company. During the panel, the questions and answers centered on our career development and challenges to get to the success we had so far.

After the panel ended, I stayed to take pictures with students and teachers, and suddenly a Hispanic student from Freeport School district on Long Island approached me. I saw excitement in her eyes, then she told me, "This is one of the best days in my life. You are a Latina businesswoman! I've never seen someone like me in one of these forums before, and I'm so proud."

She asked me how I got there and told me her parents were so strict as Hispanics, and as an American she had another culture. I said, "Some people pay psychologists to get what you have for free, and you should take all the good and listen carefully. You will craft your own path taking the best from both worlds. Focus on the best part." She thanked me and said, "I will always remember we can get there and that is possible. I don't have a lot of examples in my life." I will always have this moment in my heart. "This right here is my purpose!" I said. I love providing hope and guidance to others through my life journey, and especially to my community, to transform lives and help others succeed!

Let your purpose fuel you.

"You must find your north star... that motivates you to get up every day and do it. Build purpose into what you're doing."
—REBECCA MINKOFF, FOUNDER OF REBECCA MINKOFF APPAREL
AND FASHION, AT THE CHIEF X CONFERENCE IN NYC 2023

I've discovered that finding and crafting your life purpose takes time and sometimes is not static but more of a journey of discovery and commitment. Allow yourself to discover this new and provocative life that will fuel your entrepreneurial spirit or revive that inner flame if you are in your mid-life career, giving you a new perspective and the courage to pivot. There is no time lost or a better time than now.

CRAFTING YOUR DEFINITION OF SUCCESS

Earlier this year, I attended my son's college graduation ceremony, and this powerful message from the dean during his address to the graduates left me thinking. He said, "Don't chase other's definition of success. Define yours."

We all have unique paths, and success is a highly personal concept. What is success to you may have a different meaning to others depending on your values, purpose, and mission. The key is to have the right attitude and mindset to help you reach your objectives.

Here are three recommendations:

- Reflect on your values: Take a moment to think about what truly matters to you. Success aligned with your values will be the most fulfilling.

- Set your own goals: Don't let external pressures dictate your goals. Define what success looks like for you, both personally and professionally.

- Stay positive: Challenges are part of the journey. A positive attitude will help you navigate them.

Remember, your attitude is the compass that points you toward your version of success. Embrace, nurture, and let it lead you on a remarkable journey. As we continue to explore and make this your new lifestyle, the next chapter explores a step in this journey that is key to every successful leaper I know, and it's simple to achieve after we realize it is the way to go.

Leaper's Tip

Defining your core values

I want to share an exercise to guide you in defining your core values as a first step in this journey of becoming a leaper and develop your maximum potential.

Step one: Ask yourself these questions and give sincere answers with several words, though not sentences (i.e. love, authenticity, spirituality, honesty, integrity...).

- What are your motivators in life?
- What are your true beliefs?
- What would you *not* negotiate for billions?
- What do you believe are your foundational values?

Step two: Rank your answers in order of importance to you, not to your partner, mom, or best friend.

Step three: Select the first and second of each answer. Those are your most precious values.

Now that you have these clear, let's talk about the journey of discovering your purpose.

Defining your purpose and definition of success

Now, it is time to create your purpose and vision and tie this to the leaper you are becoming.

Your purpose is a bold sentence defining why others should follow you. Ask yourself these questions as you craft your life purpose:

1) Who do you serve? What do you do now that excites you enough?
2) Is it tied to your core values?
3) Is it coming from your true self and is emotional enough to engage others?
4) Is it filled with passion?
5) Does it embrace change and give you enough thrill to conquer?

Define your elevator pitch. This is a phrase that encapsulates your mission and vision that you can say in sixty seconds or less.

CHAPTER 11

STRATEGY #6: TAKE ACTION AND MOVE FORWARD

"Take the first step in faith. You don't have to see the whole staircase, just take the first step."

—MARTIN LUTHER KING, JR.

Now let's look closer into taking action and what stands in the way of executing the proper steps to leap out of your lane and be in charge of your destiny.

From my conversation with Kevin, acting was a key topic for him when you are stuck or need to pivot in your life and career. Kevin said, "I believe the first element of this notion of pivoting is realizing that some part of your potential or some part of what God has in store for you is not being fulfilled, and you have to do something about it."

As we continued our conversation, he highlighted how some people stay in a job that is less fulfilling or challenging enough, or the company they work for is in turmoil and lacking leadership. A lot of emotions can go on in moments like this. Also, from my own experience, moments of crisis and change are where you see the worst and best in people.

I recalled something quite important, Kevin said to me that afternoon, "I think the people who have the greatest success—because everybody gets to a pivotal moment, don't care who you are—are those who recognize, 'All right, it's time for a change.' I've seen evidence of this in my life. I've seen evidence from others, like you, Mirna, with your journey. If you're thoughtful and prayerful, God will make it obvious what you should do next. The transition is sometimes not easy, but it'll be obvious in the sense that the potential outcomes, the upside, and the gratification will be there, and you will see the light at the end of the tunnel."

I agreed with him. When things go downhill or not as expected, it is time to consider and revisit your options. Also, when things are going smoothly, revisit your position, look back at what you achieved so far, and ask yourself, "Am I falling into the complacency trap?"

According to Indeed, complacency in the workplace is when you become so secure in your work that you take potentially dangerous shortcuts in your tasks, perform to a different quality than you once did, or become unaware of deficiencies (Indeed Editorial Team 2022).

I don't know about you, but this definition is a place I don't feel I am a part of.

And complacency is the story of being "laissez-faire" with our own lives and letting things define themselves instead of being in the driver's seat.

In order to make change work in your favor and leap out of your lane, you need action and, like a good magician, plan ahead.

I follow Deborah Liu, the CEO of Ancestry.com, on several platforms for how clear she is about leadership traits and actions to support a leadership journey. She wrote an article about creating better partnerships with ourselves when taking action, titled "Stop Outsourcing to Your Future Self." She brings an exciting perspective: Your future self is the one who pays when you don't plan ahead. Your future self is the one who must deliver on everything you commit to. Your future self has to live with all the bad decisions you make today. This is true, and regardless of whether you make a wrong decision or not, if you make mistakes, your future self will appreciate you learning from them to avoid going through them again (Liu 2023).

It's time to take that driver's seat or wake up to the idea that others are making those decisions for you. Here are the six steps—"The Leaper Action Model," or as I like to call this method, the Leapers Six—you can use as a roadmap to take action in your life and move forward:

THE LEAPERS SIX ACTION MODEL

Model credit: Mirna Eusebio Lithgow

1. Be proactive.
2. Be your brand.
3. Be relentless.
4. Be fearless.
5. Be a planner.
6. Be committed.

Now, what can we do about it? A lot. Let's dive deep into each step.

1) Be proactive: Driving your life and narrative.

Seeking transformation is a constant. Active listening and observation are your allies. With that said, you gather information to use it further. As I wrote in one of the editions of my weekly newsletter on LinkedIn, *The Leapers Mindset in a Minute*, a proactive leader takes initiative, anticipates challenges, and actively shapes their destiny (Eusebio 2023).

When you are proactive, you don't wait for issues to surface. You identify potential problems early and devise solutions. Proactive leaders prioritize tasks and manage their time efficiently. They set clear goals, plan, and maintain focus, leading to increased productivity and motivated teams. Leaders who embrace change and guide their teams through it are more likely to succeed in today's fast-paced world. Proactivity is a vital trait that distinguishes exceptional leaders, helping you navigate challenges, inspire your team, and lead your organization to new heights.

Forbes recognized me in 2017 as one of the fifty most influential women in the Dominican Republic, an honor that also led to an invitation to speak at the Forbes Women Empowerment Summit in the DR for LATAM. As a panelist during a briefing session, they asked how I had achieved such heights in my career and established myself as a leader. My response drew on the key tenets of effective leadership, emphasizing the crucial role of self-awareness and the continuous pursuit of personal growth. I stressed the importance of being proactive in shaping one's narrative and meticulously planning one's life.

2) Be your brand: Have a quality seal, leaving your mark.

*"Leave your quality mark in everything
you do and everyone you meet."*

I got this quote from my mom, which is almost a directive. No matter who you are serving or talking to, big or small, the level of quality of your output is not about them but is about you. It is about your name and your brand. She will incorporate this into one of the master classes we had in our training and consulting company. She initially learned this concept of quality and building your brand from my grandmother, who had so much wisdom. She never went to school and married young. My grandfather was a respectable young man born in DR from an immigrant family coming from Augusta, Maine, USA, on a mission to establish the first US Embassy in La Hispaniola as featured in the John Bridge family genealogy chapter dedicated to The Lithgow Family (Dawson Bridge 1924, 428–429).

They loved each other dearly, had my mother and her twelve siblings, and were married for over seventy years. My grandmother Regina, a housewife, worried about everyone else, not only her home and children. My grandparents lived in the center of a town two hours away from Santo Domingo, the capital city, in a town named Monsenor Nouel, or traditionally called "Bonao," and lived there most of their lives. She was an amazing, honest, respectful, intelligent, and creative woman and I loved her dearly. She excelled in sewing, a skill she adored, and I cherished every moment spent with her whenever possible.

I always looked forward to visiting my grandparents, a childhood highlight. They lived in a small, cozy brick house on the main street with an aluminum roof and a small patio with a vegetable patch, avocados, mangos, and a cherry tree. They were not wealthy or lived in a fancy home, but it had everything you needed and much love. My grandmother understood the concept of quality, and in every meal and dessert, no matter who came and visited, she would serve them with love and the same quality. It was her signature.

She also would spend the entire year sewing dresses, shorts, and shirts for the poor, and this was a sacred activity and an act of love. She would go to every tailor shop or wherever they sell fabric and get "retazos" that were small leftover fabrics.

She would then design the clothes and coordinate the colors to create the most beautiful patterns using high-quality materials. She would do this for the poor for free. Every year, after hundreds of boxes were filled with this beautiful collection, she would pay for a truck to transport the boxes to the poorest spot in the outskirts and mountains. She would deliver them herself to ensure they get to the ones who needed them the most. Her mantra was: "No child should be without clothes or shoes ever."

It just filled my heart seeing how she would enlist my aunts, cousins, and whoever could help her throughout the year and, with her leadership, make this happen. Above all, the clothes needed to last, have the highest quality she could provide, and be a beautiful ensemble. She would not compromise her standards, no matter who wore them. As a housewife, as expected, she would run the place to ensure everyone had what they needed and give every visitor food and provisions. My grandmother from my dad's side would do the same with the neighbors.

She never complained and always found interest in putting her industrious and creative mind to work, making sure to lend a helping hand to her neighbor or anyone in need without even having the means to share what she had. She offered her prayers daily, a testament to her deep devotion and love for God. As I grew up, she was a constant presence, visiting and caring for me during extended stays that spanned several months. Her actions and words became my lessons in faith, integrity, and the importance of extending a helping hand.

Above all, her quality seal in the way of treating others and making food for others, faith, and love were her brand. My grandma Regina died at eighty-nine years old on January 2, and my grandpa Alfred died right after from a heart attack at 106 years old on February 27.

As a leaper, you must decide early on that you will subject yourself to high standards after crafting your vision and finding your purpose. There must be consistency and coherence in how you act, even if you are trying something new or have a new job, career, or venture. In every aspect of your life, this coherence will help open doors by providing people with a clear vision of who you are and how reliable you are based on the quality of your deliverables or how you conduct yourself.

From my school years up to when I started working, I took this from my grandma and my mom as a mantra, "Your brand is your quality seal," to the extent that it is a phrase I constantly use, and my teams will know.

Always have high-quality standards as part of building your name and your brand, and be consistent.

3) Be relentless: Don't give up. Mistakes and mishaps fuel success.

"La toalla se tira solo en la playa." In English: Drop the towel only at the beach.

This is my rallying cry.

If you had been part of my team, you would know this phrase and the following ones in this chapter. When you are a leaper, you are exposed to constant change, and if no change comes your way, you will seek a new challenge and make change happen and work for you. This means you will face challenges multiple times. Some people would ask, "Why be that insane and put yourself into situations that constantly require you to leave your comfort zone?" The answer is simple. Every time you experience a challenging situation, you go through it and problem-solve. You are now prepared for the following challenge. And believe me, they will come.

Never give up, especially when betting on yourself. Think about circumstances you have gone through in your life. You have been able to conquer them and get out of them as a stronger person, 100 percent of the time. It may not always be the exact outcome you expected or wanted, but you pulled through, and it made you stronger as a parent, student, teacher, leader, partner, and as a person.

One day, we headed for a meeting at the Long Island City office with our chief operating officer to present our marketing plans for B2B, and the teams, including our finance partners at the time, were given a specific format and content to present. As some of you may have experienced in your corporate lives or at school, the content and format for the presentation were there, yet the chief operating officer had another perspective on the in-depth information he needed. Somehow, this information did not get to us in this way.

It was a disappointing meeting for my team and me. We had put many hours into it, and we could feel the frustration from the finance team as well. The chief operating officer looked at my new boss and me and said, "I know you have a lot of information. Can you come back tomorrow and share the changes?" I looked at my team, and we all had the determination in our faces to prove we could do it. I said, "We can do it. We'll be back tomorrow afternoon with this completed." I knew we could do it. My team knew I wouldn't commit or ask them if not.

My team also knew I would only ask them to do extra work with an actual situation requiring a sense of urgency. By then, I also knew how fearless and bonded we were as a team, not by chance but by design. From those three years of working together, the team grew as a driving force of excellence for the business division.

It was a marathon turnaround, and we did it! After a successful presentation, they approved the budget. We had more than needed as a backup. The job was done! I was proud of the work done and of the team. This gave us a sense of unimaginable bonding and accomplishment.

After the meeting, my boss asked, "Mirna, how did you and the team do it? You guys pulled through and did an excellent job!"

I told him, "No coincidence here—we wouldn't give up. And remember, what doesn't kill you makes you stronger." He laughed.

I have seen many examples of never giving up and being relentless. I want to share a story I usually use in my team activities.

The Panyee Football Club, as explained by a Euronews article, is a remarkable example of resilience and ingenuity, epitomizing the spirit of never giving up, regardless of the circumstances. In the tiny floating village of Koh Panyee, Thailand, a group of children, driven by their passion for football, overcame the lack of space by building their own floating football pitch. This extraordinary and innovative solution is a testament to their love for the game, symbolizing their ability to adapt and innovate in the face of limitations. The club's journey from playing on a makeshift pitch to competing in national tournaments—which they won—is a powerful example of how determination and teamwork can turn dreams into reality. Up to three thousand tourists visit the island daily, and most head straight to the floating football pitch, generating extra money for the community (Ward et al. 2023).

Don't give up despite the odds not being in your favor.

4) Be fearless: Confront fear, not the absence of fear.

Being close to customers, especially front-line employees, in any organization I work for is vital to me. I need to go to the call centers, retail shops, and field technicians' departments, meet people, and get their perspectives and ideas. I found this was the only way to learn and know the heart of a business. After I started as the head of products and marketing, this was my first action, and I keep at it even today.

I recall my second visit to our offices in Plano, Texas, and I also had to travel to visit my other team in the Tyler location. For years, I've always feared driving a car long distances on highways and interstates. I promised myself to overcome this fear there and then. The time had come, and I travelled alone this time to our Plano office, and I intended to visit the teams in Tyler, Texas, and get there by driving myself.

I rented a car at the airport and drove to the Plano office. At this time, I realized that Texas's max speed was seventy-five miles per hour, probably the maximum speed I've tried before. I took the car and started driving, enjoying the gorgeous immensity of this state. Everything is so big in Texas. The highway and its structure showed the growing infrastructure across Plano, with new businesses moving to the area. As I drive down the highway, I noticed the cars started passing me along at almost 100 miles per hour. I thought, *Wow, that's fast!*

As I drove my rented compact car, I had to hold onto the steering wheel real tight every time a car passed, but I got through it and arrived at the Tyler office feeling good about conquering my Texas highway fear. I also had to return to Dallas the same way. I learned never to rent a compact car on a Texas highway. The next time, it will be a truck!

Why was this so critical? I conquered a two-hour drive on a highway, whereas others do that daily. I had a preconceived fear to conquer, which posed a challenge for me, and it felt great when I did it.

The most important of all is that to solve bigger or more complex problems, I need to start small, and I've found that every little detail builds me to get better at it. When the more considerable challenges come, I am trained and prepared to problem-solve and have the strength to face it.

5) Be a planner: Plan, be flexible, and adapt.

Planning is essential to managing challenges ahead of them turning into bigger issues. I have learned that even though planning is necessary, since it allows you to have that blueprint for achieving your goals, being flexible in these times is equally important. There will always be headwinds your way or an unplanned situation that will come up, and being open to do things differently or in a different timing is a trait we all want to have.

Let go of something today that isn't serving you or your purpose, and that will make time for other actions that will take you there. Letting go is not easy, but part of acting as a leaper is to learn how to let go. This means you must also open yourself up to the new and not look back. There is a great exercise called the "start, stop, continue," explained in an article by Madelaine Miles, that helps you prioritize work aligned with your mission and vision, and what you should get rid of, what you should keep on doing, and what you should start doing (Miles 2023).

Consider Elain, a successful advertising and marketing executive turned solopreneur who came to America from Brazil at age sixteen due to her parents' work. She is also of Jewish descent. From the beginning, she felt different, navigating her new world by getting into college at University of California at Chapel Hill. When I interviewed Elain, I thought it was fascinating how she was able to navigate and get herself into corporate America. She evolved from an advertising agency to sales marketing at NBC Universal, from a mid-management position at Young and Rubicam, to a VP leadership role at AMC Networks working with some of the most iconic shows such as *The Walking Dead* and *Mad Men*, and managing first-of-its partnerships with brands such as Mountain Dew. Now with her own company supporting clients such as NBC Universal, Elain is one of the most authentic leaders I know, and she was part of my cohort in Class 39 from the Betsy Magness Leadership Program from the Women in Cable and Telecommunications (WICT) Network.

We agreed to meet via Zoom, and the instant I saw her, I felt a great connection and camaraderie as always. From our conversation, she revealed how she defined her purpose and plan based on establishing her definition of success. Also, from her perspective, it is essential to follow your gut feeling: "If you don't follow your own intuition, you then end up making decisions that are either about money or your passions, not both. It is a muscle you must work."

When deciding which projects she gets involved with, she advises, "Always look at every opportunity as another stock in your bucket. It must align with your values and definition of success and what your gut feeling is telling. If not, it won't work. "

The only time you look back is to see how far you've come and learn from your growth and glow moments.

6) Be committed: Commit to yourself and your cause. If you don't, who will?

"The date will come. We do not postpone the inevitable."

This is another of my rally cries.

You have a target or a date set, and the date will arrive no matter what. Time doesn't stop.

One of my closest friends and dear mentors I have the privilege and honor to have is my dear friend in faith, Miguel. This phrase came from him in one of our endless conversations when we were talking about self-improvement and leadership, and he was guiding me through challenging situations at work or in life in general. "Time doesn't stop. Take care of it now!"

Miguel, who I consider a mentor, is an accomplished CEO and founder in the insurance and travel assistance business, with branches in several countries and provides support to travelers worldwide. For him, a plan can be flexible, and setting dates is the key to bringing us to that sense of urgency to commit and do it. This reminds me of a phrase I said while interviewing on the *Dejando Huellas* podcast (Díaz 2023).

If you have a date set, your dreams will turn from just ideas into reality. If not, that is just what they are: dreams.

I met Liz Elting in New York City in the fall of 2023 at the Bold Table Leaders Collective event. she is the founder and CEO of The Elizabeth Elting Foundation, and she is a New York-based entrepreneur, business leader, and bestselling author. She had just released her new book *Dream and Win Big: Translating Passion into Purpose and Creating a Billion-dollar Business.* We were seated almost right next to each other. She looked stunning while wearing a beautiful red sequin jumpsuit, and we immediately clicked. I appreciated her being approachable and authentic, providing guidance drawing from her experience.

Then, she went to address the more than forty women executives present that night, talked about how to create an empire in the translation business as a founder of TransPerfect, and recommended setting up a plan and working every day to make it a reality. She also recommended above all to always have a clear contract between the parties and partnerships involved. She experienced it herself when she wanted to part ways with her cofounder. I recommend reading her book if you are starting a business.

In her book, she shares this life lesson I feel is most applicable for a leaper: "Never forget you are your own greatest resource. When you work harder than most, the world is there for the taking... and then, the changing" (Elting 2023, 321).

If you are thinking about changing jobs, or have been recently promoted, or took a new job in another company, or even creating your new venture, read *The First 90 Days* by Michael D. Watkins—a recommended title by my husband before starting his new job. It has been a companion with practical advice on what to do to set yourself for success when making these types of changes in your career. In the book, Michael invites us to prepare ourselves for a journey, not a destination. "You will have to work constantly to ensure that you are engaging with the real challenges of your new position and not retreating to your comfort zone" (Watkins 2013).

Remember, turning ideas into action requires consistent effort, perseverance, and adaptability. Combining effective leadership strategies with personal motivation can increase your chances of successfully executing your ideas.

Leaper's Tip

Let's take action. You take action and don't leave it to something to happen or someone else to help you start. You will also need others along the way because you can't do it alone. Be careful of not standing in your own way.

Let's work together on your blueprint to meaningful change and accelerate success in your life.

Self-awareness inventory: Assessing your current state
- Cultivate self-awareness through reflection and introspection.
- Reflect on your current situation, strengths, and areas for improvement.
- Conduct a self-assessment to understand your values, interests, identity, and passions.
- Practice self-compassion through exercises, or depending on your needs, seek professional guidance.

Self-reflection: Exploring your purpose and goals
- Explore techniques such as journaling, mindfulness, or self-assessment tools. Define your purpose and set your goals and objectives.
- Define clear and specific goals aligned with your growth aspirations.
- Break down long-term goals into smaller, achievable objectives. I call these the "small victories" fueling us to continue delivering.
- Ensure goals are measurable and have a timeline with specific dates to track progress effectively.
- Develop your definition of success. What does it look like for you?

Create a personal growth plan

- Develop a personalized action plan outlining steps and milestones. Use the "Leapers Six" steps to guide you.

- In order to prioritize, use the "keep, stop, continue" exercise to define what you will get out of your plate, what you will continue to invest time in, and what is in process that should stay on course. I recommend the detailed methodology that Madeline Miles presents in her article "Start, Stop, Continue" for Better Up. You can also find others on the web.

- Determine the resources and support you will need for your growth journey.

- Prioritize tasks and allocate time for learning, practice, and self-reflection.

CHAPTER 12

STRATEGY #7: CHANGE AS YOUR LIFESTYLE

"Change is hard at first, messy in the middle, and gorgeous at the end."
—ROBIN SHARMA

One of the things my husband and I love to do the most is exercise outdoors. We love hiking as a family and enjoy the time together, and Long Island brings such fantastic scenery most of the year and trails to go with the running streams and breathtaking views of the Long Island sound.

One day I told my husband, "I don't think I can go hiking today. Let's go for a run around the neighborhood."

He agreed. "Sure, I see Peloton has an outdoor option with guided classes. Let's give it a try."

We started an outdoor class with my favorite Peloton instructor, Robin Arzón. I just found her so real. She has "Latina" roots, an excellent music selection, and a way to connect with people and coach you through the class that's unique. Her story of getting into running is amazing. As she explains on her website, she decided from being a lawyer to change careers and turn to a job in fitness and wellness. She is now a successful executive, Peloton elite instructor, a celebrity managing her brand platform, and a multiple-times published author. She is a leaper and a motivator of change in people's lives. What an example of leaping out (Arzón 2023)!

What happens when we realize change is needed in our lives and thinking about it makes us feel better? Change is a constant, a reality of life, and making it a lifestyle can transform you into that powerhouse that averts a challenge and creates an opportunity out of it. While I have had many conversations with incredible executives, students, teachers, and family members from different generations, and through my personal experience, let me share some of the findings on how leaping out of your lane can become your lifestyle and have great impact in your success story.

BELIEVING IN YOURSELF AND YOUR ABILITY TO EMBRACE CHANGE

Being a leaper implies you will seek change, see challenges as opportunities, and make this part of your lifestyle. This will require you to know your story and purpose and have clearly defined values and beliefs.

This sense of purpose and your values are a compass that helps you navigate through moments of uncertainty in your life and clearly understand what you are unwilling to negotiate or lose, no matter the circumstances.

They also help you stay grounded and keep your authenticity while seeking changes, taking new challenges, or exploring uncharted waters.

Stay true to yourself. You are going to need it all the way.

Cultivate a mindset that believes in your abilities to turn ideas into action.

Build self-confidence and overcome self-doubt by recognizing your strengths and past successes. You will find out how many extraordinary accomplishments you had so far and how many learnings have come from your most difficult moments.

Believing in yourself is a fundamental aspect of personal growth and success, as well as accepting new challenges and leaping out. It involves having confidence in your abilities, trusting your judgment, and maintaining a positive mindset. When you believe in yourself, you are more likely to take risks, persevere in facing challenges, and reach your full potential. This is easier said than done and is a process that takes time and courage.

AVOID SELF-SABOTAGE AND PERFECTIONISM

I self-doubted myself in the early years of my career, and I went from being a mobile sales door-to-door agent all the way up to manage a $10 billion product portfolio in corporate America. Self-sabotage is a self-defeating behavior that can hinder personal growth and success. It often manifests as undermining one's efforts, holding oneself back from achieving goals, and engaging in negative thinking and behavior patterns.

Self-sabotage can take various forms, such as procrastination, self-doubt, fear of failure, and engaging in self-destructive habits. As renowned author and speaker, Brené Brown, emphasizes in her book *Daring Greatly*, "If we want freedom from perfectionism, we have to make the long journey from What will people think? to I am good enough" (Brown 2015, 130–131).

Perfectionism will lead you to a fixed mindset. Break the spell. We are enough.

My mom has a famous and straightforward expression in her household: "Polarize everything negative you do or say that comes in your way." She believes when negative thoughts come our way, we polarize by thinking of the positive side. This has come in handy for me and can also help you.

DARE TO TAKE A NEW CHALLENGE AND DO THINGS DIFFERENTLY

Open yourself to constant learning, curiosity, exploration, flexibility, and adaptability. This will open opportunities and help you see clear paths for growth and achievement. Invest in self-improvement by acquiring new knowledge and skills relevant to your ideas or area of interest. You should also always have a roster of interesting books you can read about topics you need to understand or set an opinion on. This will open your mind to new ways of thinking.

I encourage you to seek mentors, attend workshops, and network with like-minded individuals to expand your knowledge base. Be strategic about why you want to incorporate this change in your life or why you want to seek this new venture. Keep your vision and purpose as a compass to evaluate if this new step will get you closer to your objective and fulfill your purpose.

I'm a technology advocate, passionate about enhancing knowledge and performance with the newest technology available and what this can bring to people and organizations to realize their full potential. You can also use these new tools and resources around you to help you enhance your performance, understand your new challenge better, and manage change in your favor.

ChatGPT was released in November 2022 as a generative artificial intelligence tool that provides a new way to support research, produce content, and even generate images. It's now become mainstream. At this point, a third of white-collar workers have used it, according to a *Time* article. As artificial intelligence and generative AI tools evolve and are readily available, this will change as you read how we work, produce content, and go on with our daily lives. We would have to relearn this change and adapt to thrive (Constantz 2023).

I asked Daisy Expósito-Ulla for an interview as a dear friend and successful executive, whom I admire for her work and the impressive multiple accolades she has received. She is a recognized authority in multicultural marketing communications who is widely credited as one of the pioneering architects of the US Hispanic Market. She has the distinctive honor of having been inducted into no less than The American Advertising Hall of Fame of the American Advertising Federation.

She is chairman/CEO of D expósito and Partners, the ad agency chosen in 2015 as the AEF Agency of the Year by the Advertising Educational Foundation, which recognized Daisy "for her contributions to American advertising." Before founding the company she now leads as chairman/CEO of Young and Rubicam/WPP's The Bravo Group (now VML), she helped launch and subsequently build it to become the largest US Hispanic ad agency in history.

She is a visionary, a creative mind, and a powerhouse with a transformational career working with brands such as AT&T, McDonald's, Kraft Foods, Sears, Unilever, Pfizer, Bank of America, and AARP. She has also been regarded as a substantive instrumental player for her role in helping the US Census engage US Latinos, both in 2000 and 2010.

Her contributions exemplify how we can bring change, transformation, and success into a sector and community such as Hispanics in America. I also recognize the characteristics of a leaper in her, as she went on to create—almost "invent"!—a new category or niche and, as a result, build a brand from scratch.

When we started our video call, the first thing I notice as a Latina is how well put and beautiful her make-up is—with bright red in her lips and a gorgeous matching turtleneck. We talked about her early career starting as a creative writer at the small office space Bravo had at the time within Y&R/NY.

It quickly became apparent how her entrepreneurial spirit helped her "leap" to manager of that deceivingly small unit that would later become a gigantic company of great influence and success, to the point that it provided the blueprint for the multicultural industry. "I asked for the position, and they didn't mind giving it to me since in those days nobody would have expected Bravo's growth to explode like it did!" she tells me without a trace of bragging. It is evident that she created her own business model and proved right.

She admits change is a constant in her life and insists transformation is essential to succeed. It's an opportunity to reinvent. It comes with the ability to pivot. Technology is constantly changing, and we need to adapt to win in the marketplace.

I asked Daisy what has been one of her biggest challenges and how she would pivot to greater success with her agency. "Undoubtedly, during the COVID-19 pandemic, everything changed. We had no idea if we would live, if the agency would survive, and we were resourceful by using technology in our favor. We made business pitches online. We grew in the healthcare area by providing much-needed education and communication to Hispanics during those difficult times. We were there to help the community. It made our business stronger, and I became more resilient. If a door is closed, build a tunnel to go through!"

Daisy also reflected on how they are constantly experimenting with changes in technology. "We were one of the first multicultural agencies to use programmatic media buying, now incorporating artificial intelligence to innovate and stay current. However, as a leader, our most important assets through life and through changes are our people.

"I have exceptional talent collaborating with me and the teaming of my lifetime partner and husband, Jorge Ulla, a businessperson and an award-winning filmmaker, who is our agency cofounder." The couple has been individually recognized with the FACE Award (Facts About Cuban Exiles), which is arguably the most prestigious recognition among Cuban-Americans. "It's the human factor that always wins in the end," Daisy adds with conviction.

For a few minutes, the conversation departed a bit from the focus of this book as she spoke about her family with pride: her son, Gabe, a writer and bestselling author; her daughter, Martha, a photographer; her college grad grandkids; nephews and nieces. I then asked Daisy—the "success story," the wife, the mother—what message or tips she would give to people with an entrepreneurial heart seeking that push to take a leap. "First of all, know what you want and know that you can do it. Do the groundwork. Be ready to work harder than anyone next to you. Sweat counts! Be vocal. Embrace your culture and who you are. Learn, ask, and listen. Be honest. And be yourself!"

Doing things differently, adapting to change, planning, and taking a leap by starting something new helped her achieve the successful business she has today. Leaping out of your lane really pays off!

What else that is different and challenging will you do for your team, your business, your community, or yourself?

Will you start small and take a different route, train, or car one day instead of doing the same daily routine? If you don't try, you won't know if there is a new place across that path you didn't know existed, and now you want to know.

Will you say "Yes!" to that invite or be part of that new group in your class, work, neighborhood, or church that will expand your circle?

Will you be willing to break silos between two departments at work and be the person who says "Yes!" to that new project to work cross-functionally?

Start small, though some of you might even say these are not small changes. Ask yourself what you can do.

Make a list of your daily routine.

What will you change to make it more interesting and different?

What will you stop doing?

When was the last time you tried something spontaneous and new?

BE A NON-CONFORMIST, ASK QUESTIONS, AND LET GO

By having a flexible mindset and being open to new ideas, individuals can cultivate a deeper understanding of the world and foster innovative solutions to complex problems. It is also about letting go if needed and not just keeping an idea not serving you. As Adam Grant, organizational psychologist at The Wharton School and a number one *New York Times* best seller, posted, "Refusing to give up on a failing plan is not an act of resilience. It's a display of rigidity. Grit is not about persevering with a route that isn't working. It's about staying focused on a goal but flexible on the path" (Grant 2023).

When you are passionate about something, your focus and energy are on making this a reality. You must be a true believer and assess if this aligns with your purpose and if your core values are worth fighting for. Incorporating this self-reflection in everything you do will become a habit in your daily life.

You can also break your idea into smaller, manageable tasks. This prevents feeling overwhelmed and allows you to tackle one step at a time, gaining momentum.

When you have new ideas or an unattainable goal, you must break it into smaller pieces to understand and address it better. As a family, we have a mantra that helped my husband and me through moments when we didn't make wise financial decisions or had changed jobs, creating financial distress in the family. We will think:

If you can't solve the month, solve the week, if not the day, if not the hour, if not this very second.

This applies to any situation in life. If you feel overwhelmed and think about how much you need to get done, apply this concept and it will get you unstuck.

REBUILD YOUR HABITS

"Early to bed, early to rise, makes a man healthy, wealthy, and wise."
—BENJAMIN FRANKLIN (BOSTON TEA PARTY SHIP 2023).

In order to leap out of your lane, you need to have the strength of an athlete. This doesn't mean you must have all aspects covered at once. You must build your mind and body strength to become a successful leaper. They will develop in time.

Develop self-discipline	Cultivate the habit of self-discipline by setting clear priorities, managing your time effectively, and staying focused on your goals. You can avoid procrastination and create a routine that supports your productivity. Even if you procrastinate sometimes, don't beat yourself up. Maybe it was what you needed at the time, based on your circumstances. There will always be a new chance of doing things differently and better.
Seek feedback	Could you share your idea with trusted people who can provide constructive feedback and valuable insight? Incorporate their perspectives to refine your idea or your opportunity for improvement and increase its chances of success.
Take calculated risks	Assess the potential risks and rewards of pursuing your idea and be willing to take calculated risks. Embrace the possibility of failure as a learning opportunity and develop resilience to bounce back. Being a leaper is not a synonym for being unprepared but is planning and thinking strategically and with intentionality.

Stay motivated	Find intrinsic and extrinsic sources of motivation to sustain your drive. Set personal rewards for achieving milestones and remind yourself of your idea's positive impact on your life, on your career, and for others. Discover new personal interests just for you, your "me time," from reading a new book to trying a new sport that creates a new circle of friends or a new problem-solving method for you.
Stay healthy	Through moments of change, your body and mind will experience levels of stress, and you need to counteract by preparing your body, mind, and emotions to keep you from burning out. Prioritize yourself, even if this means you will be working hard. Still, you will find time. Start with small victories of a twenty minute walk and then gradually increase the level of exercise, seeking support or coaching if you need healthier food habits or counseling if you need professional assistance with your emotions and emotional intelligence. Don't try to fit into a strict routine if you are starting. Just find a way to create consistency in what you are doing through the period you are living in your life. That is what gives you long-term and sustainable results.

As our kids went into college, we found ourselves with additional time and a prioritized agenda around what we wanted to do. With this came the idea to start writing classes and getting into a program to write this book. I leaped out of my lane again as an author, adapting to this new life change of seeing our kids grow independent. My husband and I have been married for more than twenty years, and since we started at a young age, we have benefited from spending more time together so we can enjoy life, feeling like the two teenagers who fell in love years ago.

Leaper's Tip

Below is an exercise to help you identify what you need to become a leaper or incorporate change into your life. If you are already experiencing change, take advantage of the opportunity to self-reflect on where you are and enhance or build your blueprint.

Step 1) Develop new habits: You can use a habit-tracking system and accountability mechanisms to keep you on track.

- Which habits do you need to change or redirect to that support your personal growth and well-being?
- What do you need to stop doing to have more time available for actions that will bring you greater success?
- Please take a look at your routine. Are you on autopilot?
- Which strategies can you implement for habit formation and behavior change?

Step 2) Define a game plan for overcoming challenges and obstacles: You need to create resilience and a strong support system around you.

- Which are the potential challenges and barriers to your personal growth?
- Which strategies can you develop to overcome obstacles and setbacks?
- What is your level of resilience, and what do you need to incorporate a growth mindset to navigate challenges effectively?

Step 3) Be open to learning a new skill and adapt:
Technology, people, and processes will keep evolving, and
any of them should outpace you. Be strategic and tie this
to your vision and purpose.

- Could you identify skills and knowledge areas relevant
  to your personal growth goals?
- Could you create a learning plan to acquire or deepen
  new skills?
- Explore various learning resources, such as books, courses,
  mentors, or online platforms.

Step 4) Build a support network:
- Engage in networking activities or join relevant groups
  to connect with like-minded individuals.
- Which individuals or communities can provide support
  and encouragement?
- Can you identify mentors, coaches, or accountability
  partners to guide your growth journey?

Step 5) Be a constant learner:
- Read books or listen to audiobooks. Choose books related
  to personal development, leadership, or the skills you want
  to acquire. Set aside dedicated time each day or week for
  reading. Be intentional about it.
- Attend webinars, workshops, or seminars. Look for online
  or in-person events that offer learning opportunities and
  sign up for sessions relevant to your interests and goals.
- Engage in online courses or e-learning platforms. Enroll
  on Coursera, Udemy, or LinkedIn Learning to acquire
  new skills or deepen your knowledge in specific areas
  of interest.

Step 6) Monitor and evaluate progress:

- Regularly assess your progress and evaluate the effectiveness of your growth efforts.

- Adjust goals, strategies, and action plans based on feedback and results.

- Celebrate milestones and achievements along the way.

- Self-reflect on being in your comfort zone or if the activity still challenges you. If not, it is time for change.

CHAPTER 13

STRATEGY #8: LEAPER'S CHEERLEADERS: DEFINE YOUR TRIBE

"Surround yourself with only people who are going to lift you higher."
—OPRAH WINFREY

REDEFINING YOUR CIRCLE

Every time you go through changes, you enrich your circle of people who can influence and propel your cause or success.

The quality of your closest friends and allies can have a direct impact on supporting your success. They can impact your mental health, energy level, and even happiness. Choose wisely who you let in that circle and who you allow to have that impact on you. We come again to that point when we reflect on our choices, and since they are choices, we have the choice in our hands to pivot.

As cited in an article by the National Library of Medicine, Albert Einstein once said, "Stay away from difficult people—they have a problem for every solution." This explains by itself how the people who you surround yourself with will uplift you or be a deterrent in your path to greater success (Neirotti 2021).

Every leader I have interviewed or worked for has had a circle of influence and their own personal board of directors. I for sure have mine.

This not only helped these executives get to where they got to, but they also had others who believed in them or were their sponsors. I prefer to use the word "sponsor" instead of "mentor" since a sponsor is someone who will root for you even when you are not present in the same room. It's a commitment that goes beyond mentoring. I've personally seen a big difference.

As my Latin roots will confirm, I am a social person. I love to connect with others, understand the stories behind their choices and their development, and understand how I can impact their lives and make them better. I need that Latin "calorcito," which means a warm and cozy feeling of belonging and wanting us here.

After starting our US journey, connecting with people outside work and school proved challenging for us, casting a shadow of loneliness. In the Dominican Republic, we actively engaged in the business community, hosting parties and get-togethers with family and friends. Our involvement extended to community institutions, chambers of commerce, and church ministries supporting couples and families. Those connections, that community of like-minded friends, continue to root for us from a distance no matter where we are.

Feeling the need to replicate this sense of community in the US, I set out to find my tribe, a group of like-minded individuals, and a circle of trust. Work presented an opportunity to apply for the Women in Cable Telecommunications' Betsy Magness Leadership

Institute Program (BMLI), a leading program for women in the tech, media, and cable industry, to accelerate my connections and industry presence. My involvement in various activities, courses, and luncheons has already led to meeting exceptional executives and receiving awards for impacting the industry.

I successfully navigated the rigorous BMLI application and interview process, earning a place in Class 39. The acceptance letter sent me jumping with joy. It signified the start of a year filled with growth and real transformational leadership experiences. It introduced me to a community of empowered, high-performing, and caring women leaders, each a powerhouse in her field. We became each other's cheerleaders, sharing joy, support, and genuine care. In this active community, I've experienced growth, change, boldness, and resilience.

Seeing the power of community motivated me. Fast forward six years later, I became part of a founding member of CHIEF, a community to empower and elevate women into positions of power. That is the power of your circle and how it reflects in your life. Also that year, my achievements in the business segment received multiple awards in the industry that elevated women, minorities, and cable and telecom executives.

Through supporting your community and your tribe, they support you back as well and make you a stronger person or leader. I now serve on the Board of the Long Island, New York Chapter of the American Red Cross. Seeing the love and dedication of so many volunteers in the community who want to do good and serve others is just inspiring and is also aligned with my purpose in life of helping others and my beliefs.

I asked my dear friend Jessica Gleason, VP head of Courageous Studios for Warner Bros Discovery, for a conversation about our experience at BMLI and to talk about her career journey where she had to pivot. We met via Zoom, and Jessie—what we call her—had gorgeous red hair and was always smiling.

She recounted how after graduating from Northeastern, she started as a receptionist at an production firm in Boston that eventually went out of business. She wanted to stay in Boston, so she went to work for a shop at Copley Plaza Mall and became an assistant manager until her next opportunity took her back into the entertainment industry.

Some friends she knew called her for an opportunity at a video craft agency as a lateral move, which she took. "I lobbied myself to the operations manager position when my former boss left, and they decided to give me what they call a 'sink or swim' opportunity. I was operations manager there for the next three or four years, and then I wanted to really move to New York City and go after something bigger."

She went to find an opportunity as the head of production at a New York City boutique production company called Beehive. She was then recruited to work for the Sundance channel, which was partly owned by Robert Redford and was the independent television expression of the Sundance Film Festival. "I thought what a best-of-both-worlds scenario to work in television but for filmmaking and independent storytelling. It was not a move up. It was a lateral move in, or some might even say that the title was reversed or backward. But it was on a much larger platform, larger stage, higher stakes, and for more money. I learned how to launch streaming shows and products simultaneously with the television series with hit shows such as *The Walking Dead* and *Better Call Saul*," Jessica said.

Jessica's biggest challenge was when AMC Networks and Sundance became one team. The AMC team had long been there and were at the birth of the cable-scripted drama golden age when they launched *Mad Men* and *The Walking Dead*. That team had a lot of experience with audiences of up to twenty million people watching those shows, and when the business started to change, they looked at overlapping roles and the need to consolidate.

"I saw they were bringing us together and that there was going to be an opportunity for the future that if we could do this well, not only would it be a good opportunity for me but my boss and my colleagues. But it was a terrifying time. There was one conversation I remember vividly where one of those individuals told me, 'I know what your intentions are and that you're trying to do good. What you want to do is never going to work. This place is so complicated. I've tried that before, and it didn't work. You won't be able to do it,' he said. And I said to him, 'Well, I have to try.'"

And so she did for her team, colleagues, and company. That unity and courage brought them together to a common goal and success. We both learned in Betsy Magness Leadership Institute that when you're ruminating about conversations, you must silence the noise, do what you're good at, and know that you don't have to have everything perfect. You just have to try.

To create a sense of community or teams, the most important element you need is trust.

"When a recruiter came to me from Warner Media, looking for a head of the production for their in house branded content studio called Courageous, which was the brand studio designated to the CNN audience, I said yes and interviewed, and here I am." She jumped into opportunities and went through many challenges, but she kept close to her team through the changes in each of these new opportunities. She took them by the hand and ensured they were tight through the noise or the uncertain moments. We can also call that sense of unity in teams a support community that are a leaper's cheerleader.

"And if you bring authenticity, you really can't go wrong. With change, you can't go fast. You must pace yourself, be very thoughtful, and try one thing at a time rather than try to take it all on yourself. I've really had to learn to pace myself and choose certain things that I want to try and help and prioritize," Jessica concluded.

The conversation with Jessica reminded me of the wisdom behind the words of the trailblazer Ruth Bader Ginsburg, associate for the Supreme Court of the United States of America, or pop culture name Notorious RBG, "Fight for the things that you care about. But do it in a way that will lead others to join you" (American Writers Museum 2023).

LEANING INTO YOUR COMMUNITY TO OVERCOME CHALLENGES

As I reflect on our journey as a family coming to the US, we had a clear objective and a fulfilled one. The experiences and challenges we had as a family in the venture had made us stronger and had further enabled our capacity to think that everything is possible if we have faith, stay true to our beliefs and ourselves, and put in the effort to make it happen.

As I leaped out to this unknown, I achieved greater success than I imagined, now as an author of a book and becoming the CEO of my own technology and consultancy company, with more to come as our journey just started.

Our tribe has expanded cross-countries and geographies through a multi-cultural experience that has marked our family for good forever. We put all our dreams in the hands of God, worked to make it through, and represent our Latino community as a hard-working and courageous community that never gives up following its dreams.

I am grateful for all the people in our new circles in this new country that were welcoming to our family and supported us all the way. And as I always tell my kids (young adults now), we pay it forward to help others grow, become better versions of themselves, and learn how to make change work in their favor.

When you help your team, you help a family that is behind. When you help a neighbor, you help the community and your family as a result. When you help the community, you help a country and make this world a thriving place.

Being there for others, fostering teamwork, and empowering others around you enables growth, and it also builds your tribe. They will be there for you, as you will be there for them.

Spread the good word out. Leaping out of your lane and getting out of your comfort zone is changing your life forever. Thank you for making the decision to embark on this journey of embracing change. I know your next success story is now closer, and you will get even farther to a brighter future than you ever imagined.

Being a leaper is contagious. You are now on your way of becoming one, an unstoppable force that will embrace change and make it your currency.

Change is good. Embrace it and grow.

Take the leap.

Cheers to you!

CONCLUSION

———

"At some point, however, life will inevitably complicate any dream, whether it's breaking into certain professional field, performing on a big stage, or making meaningful social change... You will need to armor up as well. If you want to break barriers and knock down walls, I've found, you'll need to find and protect your own boundaries, watching over your time, your energy, your health, and your spirits as you go."
—MICHELLE OBAMA

As this book ends, our lives continue. I want to leave you with a summarized version of the chapters as a handbook you can return to for inspiration whenever you need. This can become handy anytime, as the journey is continuous.

As the beautiful extract that introduces this chapter, a toolkit always comes in handy and is necessary to equip us for tremendous success. After our journey together, you experienced how exposing yourself to new challenges, with courage and determination, propels your life, career, and family forward.

Leapers are change makers and change agents. They see challenges and change as opportunities—a catalyst for growth. When we see the world through the lens of seeking change and evolution, embracing them will leave a positive mark in our lives.

CHAPTER 1—ARRIVAL: THE LEAPER WITHIN

Leaping out of your lane will not make your journey easier or harder. It's about taking the lead in your life and career. Take intentional and conscious steps and adapt your plan as opportunities arise. It's about exposing yourself and giving permission to your alternative life. Embracing change is essential for us to thrive. Nevertheless, our brains are wired for routine, favoring the familiar over the unfamiliar, making change harder. A new mindset needs to take place in you—a leaper's mindset.

Make change your currency and make it work in your favor by learning how to leap out to the life you never thought you had in front of you.

CHAPTER 2—HISTORY OF SUCCESS: IT IS NOT A STRAIGHT LINE

We feel safe becoming this subject matter expert and going through a repetitive known pattern.

A "leaper" sees the world through change, seeks change in their life, and transforms any situation where change is involved into an opportunity. They are masters of uncertainty, are flexible, adaptable, curious, and focused, and have a growth mindset. They manage to start from scratch or rebuild in challenging situations and moments of crisis and even come back stronger than ever.

Your career or life journey is not a straight line, and you should be intentional about your leaps.

Chapter 3—STATUS QUO: DEBUNKING "IT IS WHAT IT IS"

A leaper's purpose is also to look at the big picture and help others see it, too, leaping out to learn other parts of the business that will position them to win and be better at their current roles. That is the power of challenging the status quo and fixed mentalities. If you don't go through complex situations that bring you out of your comfort zone, you won't grow as much or be prepared for your next chapter. Your future self will be eternally grateful.

Chapter 4—THE SHOWSTOPPER: FEAR AND HOW IT CAN HOLD YOU BACK

To leap out of our lanes, learning to identify the different types of fear and how to manage them is essential. It's not about becoming a fearless person. It is about better understanding your sources of fear, having the courage to confront your fears, and working to overcome them. There could be the fear of trying something new, the fear of financial struggle, the fear of failure, the fear of perceptions of others, and the fear of exclusion. Seeking help from a coach or expert is always encouraged, as this can accelerate your process of conquering this milestone, get unstuck, managing situations of trauma and help you to move on, and start your planning to greater growth.

CHAPTER 5—THE LEAPER'S PLAYBOOK: EIGHT STRATEGIES TO EMBRACE CHANGE

The leaper's playbook uses the foundational elements we have seen so far as a basis and takes you through the steps on what shapes a leaper and how you can redirect and be more equipped for dealing with change. There are eight strategies: self-awareness and compassion; being a constant learner; grit and courage; resilience and confidence; purpose-driven life; taking action and planning; change as a lifestyle; and defining your leaper's tribe.

CHAPTER 6—STRATEGY #1: SELF-AWARENESS AND COMPASSION

The quest for self-awareness has become more essential in a rapidly changing world. Being a constant learner and understanding oneself through introspection has become a powerful personal growth and development tool. We gain valuable insights about our strengths, weaknesses, and aspirations through introspection. By examining our thoughts, emotions, and motivations, we can identify behavior patterns, limiting beliefs, and areas where improvement is needed. This self-awareness forms the foundation for initiating positive changes and better understanding ourselves.

CHAPTER 7—STRATEGY #2: GRIT AND COURAGE: PASSION, PIVOT, AND PERSEVERANCE

Grit and courage for what you believe is your passion will help you organize your life to the changes needed to achieve your goals. In life, as in business, we must be flexible enough to change our approach when needed and pivot. If something needs to be fixed or is not good enough for our purposes and goals, we must detach sometimes from our original strategy and change to a new one. Find your passion. Identify your superpowers and what it is you are good at. And have the determination and grit to leap into the life you want.

CHAPTER 8—STRATEGY #3: BEING A CONSTANT LEARNER: SHIFTING YOUR MINDSET

A growth mindset believes one's abilities and intelligence can be developed through dedication, effort, and a willingness to embrace challenges. It involves viewing failures and setbacks as opportunities for learning and personal growth. Leapers are not afraid of challenges. we use them as fuel, and if there is something we cannot manage, we will find the way. Having a growth mindset is to keep chasing that hero, that better version of ourselves, who will be thankful ten years from now that we opened our hearts and minds to learn constantly.

CHAPTER 9—STRATEGY #4: BUILDING RESILIENCE AND SELF CONFIDENCE

Resilience will help you manage difficult or challenging life experiences, especially through mental, emotional, and behavioral flexibility and adjustment to external and internal demands.

These are the three resilience types we explored in this book: emotional, cognitive, and physical. To become a leaper, you must also build a special capacity to "move on." To win, there is another essential trait we need in our tool kit, and that is self-confidence, believing in ourselves and trusting we will be able to make it.

CHAPTER 10—STRATEGY #5: A PURPOSE-DRIVEN LIFE

Leapers have a very clear sense of purpose in life, and despite the different experiences they throw themselves into, they choose to accept and gravitate to this sense of meaning and purpose.

By understanding and articulating your "why," you can create a sense of clarity, inspiration, and direction in your life. I encourage you to communicate your "why" effectively to inspire others, build trust-worthy loyal relationships, and drive meaningful change to your life inspired in your why and your values. Purpose and vision are crafted over time. Certain events can mark a new chapter and help the leaper in you resurface and prompt change to pivot. Don't chase other's definition of success. Define yours.

CHAPTER 11—STRATEGY #6: TAKE ACTION AND MOVE FORWARD

To make change work in your favor and leap out of your lane, you need action and, like a good magician, plan ahead. There are six steps you can use as a roadmap to take action in your life and move forward. I like to call this model the Leaper Action Model: be proactive, be your brand, be relentless, be fearless, be a planner, and be committed.

CHAPTER 12—STRATEGY #7: CHANGE AS YOUR LIFESTYLE

Being a leaper implies you will seek change, see challenges as opportunities, and make this part of your lifestyle. This will require you to know your story, your purpose, and have clearly defined values and beliefs. This sense of purpose and your values are a compass that helps you navigate through moments of uncertainty in your life and clearly understand what you are unwilling to negotiate or lose, no matter the circumstances. Cultivate a mindset that believes in your abilities to turn ideas into action.

CHAPTER 13—STRATEGY #8: LEAPER'S CHEERLEADERS: DEFINE YOUR TRIBE

The quality of your closest friends and allies can have a direct impact on supporting your success. They can impact your mental health, energy level, and even happiness. Choose wisely who you let in that circle and who you allow to have that impact on you. Through supporting your community and your tribe, they support you back as well and make you a stronger person or leader. Bring authenticity into your relationships and reciprocally add value to build trust.

And now it is time to depart, until we meet again. I thank you for being part of this journey with me.

Change, as time, never stops.

Leapers—keep on moving!

ACKNOWLEDGMENTS

I shared this idea of writing a book with some friends of my BMLI community five years ago at our graduation ceremony, and then this journey started. My family encouraged me to continue to pursue my dream and supported me every step of the way.

I am grateful for many great people whom God purposefully used to help me accomplish this milestone. My dear friend Eugina Jordan, who served as a conduit and introduced me to Eric Koester and his team at Manuscripts LLC. I'm thankful for my editors, marketing, and the training team: Ilia, Kristy, Shanna, Jen, Matteo, George, Anne, Jordan, Amanda and Kayla.

I appreciate my LinkedIn community, Leapers Mindset in a Minute Community, and my Instagram and Facebook followers for your support. I'm also grateful for the beta readers and their feedback; the executives who shared their stories, Kevin, Stephanie, Laura, Jessica, Elain, Claudia, Ney, Daisy, Randy, Ryan, and Wendy; and those who generously supported the crowdfunding efforts:

Ivan Aristy Ruiz	Carlos Eusebio del Rosario
Isabella Aristy Eusebio	Marigina Eusebio Lithgow
Ivan Ernesto Aristy Eusebio	Kristy Uvena
Elvira Lithgow	Ricardo Tejada

Maria Teresa Tejada
Michiko Pegeron
Audrey Navarro
Terri Gunnell
Nancy Scanlon
Monica Halperin
Sarah F. Weinstein
Dana Massey
Jackie DeFlorio
Jessica Gleason
Erika Guerra
Isaac Madera
Thais Herrera
Randy Gromlich
Angela Cruz
Anjene Abston
Zenita Henderson
Michelle Pecak
Sarah Montas-Ruiz
Carlos Tamayo
Regina Viadro
Jacqueline Mora
Firelei Pena
Haozhe Chen
Melissa Cohen
Amy Coghlan
Ukeme Awakessien Jeter
Dolores Gonzalez
Karil Taveras
Eugina Jordan
Margie Aristy
Juan Perez
Jason Cohen
Niccole Osmanski

Tony Byrnes
Laura Conde
Elain Waldman
Kristin Miata
Lou Donofrio
Elizabeth Lagrava
Chailing Ben
Michelle Guzman
Edward Villar
Phil Kull
Eric Koester
Svetlana Semenova
Emma Pilarte
Luis Castillo
Jose Mendoza
Jodie Bisono
Sara King
Beth Lind
Orlando Hampton
Savio DelPozzo
Susannah Scholl
Amelfi Almonte
Ruth Almonte
Alberto Pappaterra
Andres Oliveros
Marcela Ramirez
Julio Molina
Cayetano Chimeno
Dolores Gonzalez
Iones Rivera
Katherine Aybar
Miguel Ramirez
Josefina Morales
Victoria Thomas

Familia Cabrera Calderón
María Baez
Daniela Maini Erb
Wendy Madera
Sonja Menton
Alexis Pion
Nathalia Madera
Francisco Bertrand
Monica Williams
Karen McManus
Colleen Saringer, PhD
Carolina Camacho
Lisa Balter Saacks

Chang Wu
Deanna Senior
Ariela Nerubay
Alma Butkovic Tomac
Kathy Newberger
Anna Bertrand
Rafael Arvelo Castillo
Emma Jorge
Layi Felix
Leslie Aristy
Antonia de Aristy
Modesto Aristy

APPENDIX

CHAPTER 1

Ewing Marion Kauffman Foundation. 2022. *Who is the Entrepreneur? New Entrepreneurs in the United States, 1996–2021*. Kansas City, MO: Ewing Marion Kauffman Foundation Research.

Jamroz, Kasia. 2019. "How to Optimize the Brain's Response to Change." *Forbes Council Forum Leadership* (blog), *Forbes*. July 3, 2019. https://www.forbes.com/sites/forbescoachescouncil/2019/07/03/how-to-optimize-the-brains-response-to-change/?sh=d6b51ad449d6.

Merriam-Webster Dictionary. 2023. Definition of Change. Accessed December 21, 2023. Springfield, MA: Merriam-Webster Inc. https://www.merriamwebster.com/dictionary/change#dictionary-entry-1.

Rogers, James. 2023. "Tech Layoffs Exceed 240,000 so far in 2023, More Than 50 percent Higherinhan in All of 2022." *Computer/Electronics* (blog), *MarketWatch*. October 13, 2023. https://www.marketwatch.com/story/tech-layoffs-exceed-240-000-in-2023-a1487651.

Spector, Nicole. 2018. "How to Train Your Brain to Accept Change, According to Neuroscience." *Better by Today* (blog), NBC News. November 12, 2018.

https://www.nbcnews.com/better/health/how-train-your-brain-accept-change-according-neuroscience-ncna934011.

CHAPTER 2

Flynn, Jack, 2023. "20 Must-know Layoff Statistics (2023): Who's Being Terminated from Their Jobs." *Advice* (blog), *Zippia*. June 8, 2023. https://www.zippia.com/advice/layoff-statistics/.

Goldsmith, Kelly, Vladas Griskevicius, and Rebecca Hamilton. 2020. "Scarcity and Consumer Decision Making: Is Scarcity a Mindset, a Threat, a Reference Point, or a Journey?" *Journal of the Association for Consumer Research* 5, no. 4 (September 2020): 359, https://doi.org/10.1086/710531.

Merriam-Webster Dictionary. 2023. Definition of Scarcity. Accessed December 21, 2023. Springfield, MA: Merriam-Webster Inc. https://www.merriam-webster.com/dictionary/change#dictionary-entry-1.

CHAPTER 3

BlackPast. 2007. "(1857) Frederick Douglass, 'If There is no Struggle, there is no progress.'" *African American History* (blog), BlackPast.org. January 25, 2007. https://www.blackpast.org/african-american-history/1857-frederick-douglass-if-there-no-struggle-there-no-progress/.

Lineberry, Cate. 2006. "Diamonds Unearthed." *Science* (blog), *Smithsonian Magazine*, December 2006. https://www.smithsonianmag.com/science-nature/diamonds-unearthed-141629226/.

Mejia, Felivia. 2017. "50 Mujeres Poderosas." *Forbes República Dominicana Magazine*, May/June 2017.

Tandon, Riya. 2023. "Midlife Career Change Doesn't Have to Be a Crisis: Time to Debunk 4 Career Change Myths." *Careers* (blog), *The Economic Times*. February 20, 2023.

https://economictimes.indiatimes.com/jobs/mid-career/midlife-career-change-doesnt-have-to-be-a-crisis-time-to-debunk-4-career-change-myths/articleshow/98097195.cms?utm_source=contentofinterest&utm_medium=text&utm_campaign=cppst.

Universal Technical Institute. 2020. "Tired of Your Office Job? You're Not Alone in Seeking Career Change." *Education* (blog), Universal Technical Institute. November 12, 2020. https://www.uti.edu/blog/education/career-choices.

CHAPTER 4

Cooks-Campbell, Allaya. 2021. "Financial Stress: What's Money Got to Do with Sanity?" *Well Being* (blog), *Better Up*. October 7, 2021. https://www.betterup.com/blog/financial-stress.

Main, Kelly, and Cassie Bottorff. 2022. "Small Business Statistics of 2023." *Business* (blog), *Forbes Advisor*. December 7, 2022. https://www.forbes.com/advisor/business/small-business-statistics/#sources_section.

National Institute of Mental Health. 2023. "Specific Phobia." *National Institute of Mental Health*. Accessed December 12, 2023. https://www.nimh.nih.gov/health/statistics/specific-phobia.

Onque, Renée. 2023. "The 10 Rules of 'Ikigai,' from Authors of the Japanese Secret for a Long and Happy Life." *Health and Wellness* (blog), *CNBC Make It*. July 9, 2023. https://www.cnbc.com/2023/07/09/10-rules-of-ikigai-from-authors-of-the-japanese-secret-for-longevity.html.

Winfrey, Oprah. 2013. "Winfrey's Commencement Address." *Campus and Community* (blog), *The Harvard Gazette*. May 31, 2013. https://news. harvard.edu/gazette/story/2013/05/winfreys-commencement-address/.

CHAPTER 5

Jordan, Eugina. 2023. *UNLIMITED: The 17 Laws of a Workplace not Designed for You*. Washington District of Columbia: New Degree Press.

Scipioni, Jade. 2022. "Jessica Alba Opens Up About Building Her $550 million The Honest Company: There Were No Expectations for Me to Be Successful." *Behind The Desk* (blog), *CNBC Make It*. February 6, 2022. https://www.cnbc.com/2022/02/06/jessica-alba-on-building-honest-company-defying-expectations-therapy.html#:~:text=In%20May%20 2021%2C%20just%20days,valued%20at%20roughly%20%20%24550%20 million.

Ward, Gregory, and Manil Sethisuwan. 2023. "Meet the Football Team Floating to Success in Thailand." *Culture Series Scenes* (blog), *Euronewsculture*. February 13, 2023. https://www.euronews.com/ culture/2023/02/13/meet-the-football-team-floating-to-success-in-thailand.

CHAPTER 6

Brown, Brené. 2010. "The Power of Vulnerability." Filmed June 2010 in Houston, TX. TED video, 19:56. https://www.ted.com/talks/brene_ brown_the_power_of_vulnerability/transcript?language=en.

David, Susan. 2020. "Self-Soothing Exercises with Dr. Kristin Neff." *Checking In with Susan David*, TED. Released May 8, 2020. 21:15. https:// www.ted.com/talks/checking_in_with_susan_david_bonus_self_ soothing_exercises_with_dr_kristin_neff?autoplay=true&muted=true.

Eurich, Tasha. 2017. "Increase Your Self-awareness with One Simple Fix." TEDx MileHigh. December 19, 2017. 17:17 min. https://www.youtube.com/watch?v=tGdsOXZpyWE.

Gonzalez, Rebekah. 2022. "Taylor Swift Reveals Which Midnight's Track is Her Favorite." *iHeart Website* (blog), iHeart Music. October 3, 2022. https://www.iheart.com/content/2022-10-03-taylor-swift-reveals-which-midnights-track-is-her-favorite/.

Maruf, Ramishah. 2023. "Taylor Swift Is Now a Billionaire, Bloomberg Says." *CNN Business* (blog), CNN. October 26, 2023. https://www.cnn.com/taylor-swift-billionaire/index.html.

Neff, Kristin. 2023. "Definition of Self Compassion." *Self-Compassion* (blog). Accessed December 10, 2023. https://self-compassion.org/the-three-elements-of-self-compassion-2/.

Shonk, Katie. 2023. "The Importance of Power in Negotiations: Taylor Swift Shakes It Off." *Daily Blog Program in Negotiation* (blog), Harvard Law School. October 31, 2023. https://www.pon.harvard.edu/daily/dispute-resolution/dispute-resolution-with-spotify-taylor-swift-shakes-it-off/.

CHAPTER 7

Duckworth, Angela. 2013. "Grit: The Power of Passion and Perseverance." TED. May 9, 2013. 6:12. https://www.youtube.com/watch?v=H14bBuluwB8.

CHAPTER 8

Díaz, Ney. 2022. *Las Doce Preguntas.* Self-Published.

Dweck, Carol. 2014. "Developing a Growth Mindset with Carol Dweck." Stanford Alumni for the Graduate School of Education,

Stanford Connect. October 9, 2014. 9:37. https://www.youtube.com/watch?v=hiiEeMN7vbQ.

McConaughey, Matthew. 2014. "Matthew McConaughey Winning Best Actor | 86th Oscars (2014)." Oscars. March 11, 2014. 4:30. https://www.youtube.com/watch?v=wD2cVhC-63I.

CHAPTER 9

American Psychological Association (APA). 2018. *Definition of Resilience*. Washington DC: American Psychological Association. Updated on April 19, 2018. https://dictionary.apa.org/resilience.

Barker, Eric. 2016. "10 Ways to Boost Your Emotional Resilience, Backed by Research." *Ideas Psychology* (blog), *Time*. April 16, 2016. https://time.com/4306492/boost-emotional-resilience/.

Braun, Randi. 2022. *Something Major: The New Playbook for Women at Work*. Washington District of Columbia: New Degree Press.

Kuchel, George, Heather E. Whitson, Harvey J. Cohen, Kenneth E. Schmader, Miriam C. Morey, and Cathleen S. Colon-Emeric. 2018. "Physical Resilience: Not Simply the Opposite of Frailty." *Journal of the American Geriatrics Society* 66, no. 8 (December): 1459–1461. https://doi.org/10.1111/jgs.15233.

McDowell-Larsen, Sharon. 2021. "Fueling the Brain: From Exhausted to Energized." *Strategies for Recovery, Maintaining Focus and Boosting Brain Power*. Chicago, IL: Common Sense Leadership.

Wiseseed. 2020. "The Spirit Domain of Everyday Resilience." *Articles* (blog), *Wiseseed*. September 25, 2020. https://www.wiseseed.com/the-spirit-domain-of-everyday-resilience/.

Yap Chan, Sheena. 2023. *The Tao of Self-Confidence: A guide to moving beyond trauma and Awakening the Leader Within*. Washington DC: Wiley.

Peterson, Tanya J. 2022. "How to Improve, Increase Self-Confidence." *Self Help* (blog), *Healthy Place*. Updated March 25, 2022. https://www.healthyplace.com/self-help/self-confidence/how-to-improve-increase-self-confidence.

CHAPTER 10

Harbinger, Jordan. 2018. "Simon Sinek | What's Your 'Why' and Where Do You Find It?" *The Jordan Harbinger Show*, released February 20, 2018, video, 1 hr. 10 min. https://www.jordanharbinger.com/simon-sinek-whats-your-why-and-where-do-you-find-it/.

Harter, Jim. 2022. "US Employee Engagement Data Hold Steady in First Half of 2021." *Workplace* (blog), *Gallup*. Updated April 8, 2022. https://www.gallup.com/workplace/352949/employee-engagement-holds-steady-first-half-2021.aspx.

Herway, Jake. 2023. "To Get Your People's Best Performance, Start with Purpose." *Workplace* (blog), *Gallup*. December 10, 2023. https://www.gallup.com/workplace/350060/people-best-performance-start-purpose.aspx.

Johns Hopkins Medicine. 2023. "Mental Health Disorder Statistics." Johns Hopkins Medicine. Accessed December 12, 2023. https://www.hopkinsmedicine.org/health/wellness-and-prevention/mental-health-disorder-statistics.

CHAPTER 11

Dawson Bridge, William, ed. 1924. *The John Bridge Family in America*. Self-Published.

Díaz, Ney. 2023. "Episodio #14—Mirna Eusebio: Las Claves Del Crecimiento Profesional." *Dejando Huellas.* June 28, 2023, video, 43:55. https://www.youtube.com/watch?v=Y6jaX4EuSgg&t=1467s.

Elting, Liz. 2023. *Dream and Win Big: Translating Passion into Purpose and Creating a Billion-dollar Business.* Washington DC: Wiley.

Eusebio Lithgow, Mirna, 2023. "The Proactive Leader." *Weekly Newsletter* (blog), *Leapers Mindset-in-a-Minute.* November 7, 2023. https://www.linkedin.com/pulse/being-proactive-leader-mirna-eusebio-lithgow-xqd xe/?trackingId=X1Pj3tZ5TKu4Ow8w8z5org%3D%3D.

Indeed Editorial Team. 2022. "Complacency in the Workplace: What It Is and Tips for Changing It." Indeed. Updated June 24, 2022. https://www.indeed.com/career-advice/career-development/complacency-in-the-workplace.

Liu, Deb. 2023. "Stop Outsourcing to Your Future Self: A Guide to Getting More Done by Getting It Done Now or Not Doing It at All." *Perspectives* (blog), *Deborah Liu Perspectives.* July 06, 2023. https://debliu.substack.com/p/stop-outsourcing-to-your-future-self.

Miles, Madeline. 2023. "Start, Stop, Continue: How to Implement This Retrospective Model." *Productivity* (blog), *Better Up.* June 12, 2023. https://www.betterup.com/blog/start-stop-continue.

Ward, Gregory, and Manik Sethisuwan, 2023. "Meet the Football Team Floating to Success in Thailand." *Culture Series Scenes* (blog), *Euronewsculture.* February 13, 2023. https://www.euronews.com/culture/2023/02/13/meet-the-football-team-floating-to-success-in-thailand.

Watkins, Michael D. 2013. *The First 90 Days.* Boston, MA: Harvard Business Review Press.

CHAPTER 12

Arzón, Robin. 2023. "About Robin." Robin Arzón Sweat with Swagger. Accessed December 12, 2023. https://www.robinarzon.com/about.

Brown, Brené. 2015. *Daring Greatly.* New York, NY: Avery.

Constantz, Joe. 2023. "Nearly a Third of White-Collar Workers Have Tried ChatGPT or Other AI Programs, According to a New Survey" *Business Technology* (blog), *Time.* January 19, 2023. https://time.com/6248707/survey-chatgpt-ai-use-at-work/.

Boston Tea Party Ship. 2023. "Fun Facts About Benjamin Franklin." Boston Tea Party Ships and Museums. Accessed December 12, 2023. https://www.bostonteapartyship.com/benjamin-franklin-facts.

Grant, Adam (@AdamMGrant). 2023. "Refusing to give up on a failing plan is not an act of resilience." Twitter, May 12, 2023. 2:17 p.m.

CHAPTER 13

American Writers Museum. 2023. "Ruth Bader Ginsburg Quotes" *Ruth Bader Ginsburg* (blog) American Writers Museum. March 15, 2023. https://americanwritersmuseum.org/ruth-bader-ginsburg-quotes/#:~:text=%E2%80%9CFight%20for%20the%20things%20that,lead%20others%20to%20join%20you.

Neirotti, Rodolfo A. 2021. "The Importance of Asking Questions and Doing Things for a Reason." *Brazilian Journal of Cardiovascular Surgery* 36, no. 1 (December): 1. https://doi.org/10.21470/1678-9741-2021-0950.

LET'S STAY CONNECTED

––––––

Continue the conversation and stay connected on my social media platforms of your choice.

Websites:

www.leapoutofyourlane.com

www.mirnaeusebiolithgow.com

LinkedIn:

https://www.linkedin.com/in/mirnaeusebio/

Linktree:

https://linktr.ee/mirnaeusebiolithgow

Instagram:

https://www.instagram.com/mirnaeusebiolithgow/

Made in the USA
Columbia, SC
30 November 2024

47166545R00115